Trade and Innovation

Trade and Innovation

Theory and Evidence

Katharine Wakelin

Research Fellow, Maastricht Economic Research Institute on Innovation and Technology, University of Maastricht, The Netherlands

Edward Elgar
Cheltenham, UK • Northampton, MA, USA

Published by
Edward Elgar Publishing Limited
8 Lansdown Place
Cheltenham
Glos GL50 2HU
UK

Edward Elgar Publishing, Inc.
6 Market Street
Northampton
Massachusetts 01060
USA

A catalogue record for this book
is available from the British Library

Library of Congress Cataloguing in Publication Data

Wakelin, Katharine, 1968–
    Trade and innovation : theory and evidence / Katharine Wakelin.
    Includes bibliographical references.
    1. International trade. 2. Commerce. 3. Technological
innovations. I. Title
    HF1379.W355 1997
    382—dc21   97–22603
                                                          CIP

ISBN 1 85898 677 X

Printed and bound in Great Britain by
Biddles Limited, Guildford and King's Lynn

Contents

Tables

Acknowledgements

This book is based on my PhD thesis carried out at the European University Institute in Florence; the finishing touches were applied at INTECH and MERIT in Maastricht. Fabio Canova supervised my thesis, and despite moving between the United States, Spain and Italy gave me help, encouragement and extensive comments. I would like to thank him for everything. Other members of the Department of Economics at the EUI also deserve my thanks. Robert Waldmann read my thesis with great attention to detail and made many useful remarks; Steve Martin helped me in obtaining the data used in Chapter 6, and read early versions of some of the chapters; Louis Phlips was a constant source of encouragement. Also at the EUI, Harald Sonnberger gave me assistance with Datastream, and Jacqueline and Jessica provided unfailing good humour and the odd cup of tea. In addition, I am grateful to the European Investment Bank which financed my first two years at the institute through the Campanelli–Formentini Grant.

I would also like to thank the other members of my thesis committee: Giovanni Dosi, Jan Fagerberg and Luc Soete, for their comments. At MERIT Bart Verspagen provided the data used in Chapter 5, and many useful discussions. Other people have also given me comments during the writing of this book, they include Suma Athreye, Elena Cefis, Aldo Geuna, Nagesh Kumar and Rajneesh Narula; thank you all for your honesty. Mary O'Mahony and Nigel Pain both made useful comments on Chapter 6. INTECH and MERIT provided an excellent working environment and I would like to thank everyone who contributed to that.

On a more personal note there are a number of people who have helped to keep me sane during the ups and downs of research, especially Luis, Miguel, Jonathan, Louis, Julia, Silvia, Stefania, Valeria, Blanca, Elena and Robbin at the EUI, and Karin, Suma, Ruby, Aldo, and Rajneesh in Maastricht; I could not have done it without you. Thanks also to my family for their support throughout what must often have seemed an endless task. Finally, I would like to thank Laurence for his encouragement and limitless patience.

PART I

Technology and Trade Theory

1. Introduction

This book aims to analyse the importance of technology in influencing the trade performance of developed countries. Normally, attempts to explain this objective meet with two distinct reactions. The first reaction, that of non-economists, is that differences in technology between countries seem an *obvious* explanation for differences in trade performance, and that the importance of technology is surely not a controversial issue. The second reaction, that of most economists, is 'why technology'; how can differences in technology across countries possibly be more than a short-run phenomenon? The reason for the difference in these reactions clearly lies with economic theory which, at least as far as neo-classical trade theory is concerned, has made strong assumptions concerning technology. Neo-classical trade theory has been based on the assumption of identical technological inputs across countries, explicitly ruling out differences in technology as a source of trade. Hence the surprised reaction of most economists to the idea of considering differences in technology as a determinant of trade performance.

1.1 WHY TECHNOLOGY AND TRADE?

Despite neglecting the role of technological change in economics in the past, or its characterization as a 'black box', there is an increasing interest in understanding the mechanisms of technological change. Technology can be defined as the set of all techniques, or methods for producing a good, available to a firm. At the level of the industry or country technology is thus a collection of firm-specific technology sets (Gomulka, 1990). Technological change is the enlargement of the technology set, which may contain inefficient as well as efficient techniques; while technological progress refers only to the enlargement of the set of efficient techniques. Technology is thus an economic concept relating to techniques which are applied in an economic setting and as such can be separated from knowledge (or science) which attempts to *explain* events rather than necessarily find applications for them. Clearly the two can be closely linked, and the level of knowledge in a country can have an important impact on technology. This book is primarily concerned with technology rather than knowledge.

The proximity of an idea to an economic application can be used to classify different stages of the innovation process. Scientific research is generally interested in discovering new facts and principles and, particularly in the case of pure research, may have no economic application. Invention is the creation of a new product or production process which may never be adopted, or needs to undergo considerable changes before implementation, and thus has no automatic economic significance. Once an invention is adopted it can be described as an *innovation*, and it is this stage of the process which has most economic significance. While scientific research may be relatively independent of economic imperatives, innovation responds to economic stimuli (often termed the 'demand–pull' view of technological change) as well as to progress made by science ('technology–push'). A fourth crucial phase of the innovation process is the diffusion of innovation from the original innovator to the rest of the economy. The neo-classical approach has considered technology as a 'book of blueprints' in which the new information is codified and easily available; thus diffusion is costless and automatic. When applied to international trade theory this means that the set of techniques is assumed to be common across countries because of the perfect diffusion of information; as a result, all countries share the same production function.

An alternative view of the diffusion process sees technology as being at least partly non-codifiable (that is, tacit) and largely firm specific; this makes the transfer of technology both a costly and a complex process (Nelson, 1992). In this view of technology, innovation can give the innovating firm a specific advantage over its competitors; the level of advantage depends on the degree of codifiability and transferability of the relevant information. When this view of innovation is applied to international trade at an aggregate level, countries may have a technological advantage in some sectors which is not immediately eroded by the diffusion of technology to competing countries, giving a basis for competitive advantage. One approach to trade which is based on this conceptualization of technology as frequently firm, sector and country specific is the neo-Schumpeterian approach, which takes inspiration from the work of Schumpeter (see, for instance, Dosi et al., 1990).

This approach to technology is effective in explaining technological differences between countries, and in particular technological differences between sectors in different countries. The importance of a country's history and institutions in developing its technological profile has led to a number of studies on national systems of innovation (see, for instance, Nelson, 1993); these highlight the diverse technological strengths and weaknesses of different economies. Underlying this aggregate view of the technological strengths of sectors and countries are the firms which produce the innovations. Firms are the units in the economy which undertake most innovations and, on account of the cumulativeness and non-codifiable nature of many innovations, they are also frequently the units which benefit most from innovation. Because of the importance of firms in the innovation process, this book considers not only the role of innovation in affecting sector trade performance for different countries (Part II), but also the role of innovation in affecting firms' trade performance (Part III). The empirical literature has concentrated on the former, with only a few studies considering the role of technology at the firm level. This book aims to provide both a macroeconomic and a microeconomic study of the role of innovation in trade performance.

The role of technology in trade performance is of interest as international trade is of central importance to modern economies. International competitiveness is one of the issues which most dominates the economic agenda, and there are considerable institutional attempts to regulate international trade flows. These fall into three main groups. The first is the commitment to free trade, and the international and multilateral attempt to reduce restrictions on the free movement of goods internationally, through the General Agreement on Tariffs and Trade (GATT). The second is the integration of countries into customs unions and free trade areas, such as the European Union, and the North American Free Trade Agreement (NAFTA), which are based on the perceived benefits of free trade between a limited number of countries. The third is the area of domestic competition policy, which is increasingly becoming an arena for international dispute, and its regulation is part of the process of integration. Domestic competition policy relates to industry subsidies, the control of national wages and science and technology policy, which are all designed to protect and sustain national competitiveness. These three areas of trade policy − the control of tariffs, the creation of customs unions (and free trade areas), and the international regulation of national competition policy − remain some of the key issues for economic policy, and some of the most contentious. International trade, and international competitiveness in general, are seen as important components of the national economy which can affect domestic welfare and growth.

The significance attached to trade by economic policy makers, is due to the increasing openness of industrialized countries since the Second World

War. Advanced countries export a much higher proportion of their output than in early periods and, as a result, countries are increasingly integrated internationally, with events in foreign markets affecting the domestic market in most countries. The basis of this change has been spectacular improvements in communication which allow contact to be made easily across national and continental borders. The result of this increased integration is that small, and even medium-sized countries, are reliant on international markets for a large part of their economic transactions; and even large economies – such as the United States – are integrated with foreign markets. As a result, understanding the determinants of international competitiveness is of key importance to national economies.

The countries considered in the macroeconomic part of this book are all advanced industrialized countries at similar levels of development, and with similar real incomes per capita. However, despite this similarity in the level of income and development, the OECD countries have experienced different growth rates. One explanation for these growth differences is their varying levels of innovation, and patterns of specialization. The main hypothesis of the macroeconomic section is that technology gaps exist even between advanced countries which have similar income levels and are highly integrated. That technology gaps can persist among countries trading freely and with integrated economic systems, such as the European Union countries, indicates some salient characteristics of technology. Most importantly, it indicates that despite sharing a common scientific base, countries can still have national systems of innovation which are unique, and which reflect past experience. One implication is that economic integration and trade do not bring with them the automatic diffusion of technology; rather that technology is frequently localized, and cannot as a result be characterized as freely transferable internationally. Technological advantages remain specific, and technology gaps can be maintained between countries. The microeconomic section of the book considers the same issue at the firm level: whether differences in innovation among firms can help to explain differences in their export performance.

1.2 AN OVERVIEW

This book aims to evaluate the impact of differences in innovation on trade performance from an empirical perspective. The approach is consistent with new international economics and with a neo-Schumpeterian perspective, in that both predict that differences in innovation will play a central role in determining international trade patterns. However, the treatment of technology, and in particular the emphasis on the firm in Part III, is consistent with the neo-Schumpeterian view of technological change outlined in Chapters 2 and 6. The book combines both a macroeconomic and a microeconomic perspective on the relationship between trade and innovation.

Considerable attention is paid to the firm-, sector- and country-specific characteristics which influence the relationship between trade and innovation. The measurement of innovation, including the selection of the most appropriate proxy for technological change, and the influence of the choice of proxy on the results of the analysis, is also treated in some detail. A number of different proxies for innovation are considered, including both patent-based and R&D expenditure-based proxies, and actual counts of both innovations used and innovations produced at a sectoral level in the UK are included in the analysis.

The book is divided into four main parts. The first examines the treatment of technology in international trade theory. The development of technology in theories of trade is considered, not just in those theories which have concentrated on technology as the major determinant of trade (the so-called neo-technology theories of trade), but also neo-classical and market structure explanations for trade.

Chapter 3 of Part I follows on from the review of the treatment of technology to discuss some common features of empirical work relating differences in innovation to trade. The empirical literature is organized around three main themes: the use of a dynamic or static model of trade; whether the relationship is considered across sectors for one country or across countries for each sector; and the choice of the innovation proxy. The methodological implications of these choices are also discussed. This framework is chosen as few empirical studies (with the exception of tests of the Heckscher–Ohlin–Samuelson model) are precise tests of existing theories of trade. Rather, a number of determinants of trade are normally considered, including technology; thus attempts to classify the literature on the basis of the existing theories can be highly misleading, and a classification based on the features of the empirical model used is preferred.

Part II considers the impact of innovation on inter-country trade. It is divided into two chapters. The first, Chapter 4, concentrates on trade among four European countries. It considers the impact of differences in innovation on bilateral trade, with an extension to those countries' trade with all European countries. Simple correlations are made between bilateral differences in innovation (proxied by patents) and bilateral trade performance. The objective is to assess the extent of technology gaps between these four advanced European Union countries, both on a bilateral basis for each pair of countries, and multilaterally within Europe. The relationship is also considered for each sector across the bilateral trade flows, as large variations in the relationship are expected between European countries. Particular attention is given to how the relationship varies according to the countries and sectors involved. By considering only correlations between technology gaps and trade performance, the analysis abstracts from other determinants of trade. This reduces the explanatory power of the relationship, as differences in innovation are not expected to explain all the variation in bilateral trade performance; nevertheless it does isolate those sectors and countries for which the relationship is most important. Chapter 4 can be considered a preliminary analysis, and relates closely to Chapter 5; the latter considers the same relationship but with a more complete specification, including additional explanatory variables, and for a larger number of countries. Chapter 4 has the merit of covering a wide range of industries, including very-high-technology industries, medium-technology industries and resource-based industries.

Chapter 5 examines the relationship between trade and innovation for nine OECD countries. Additional determinants of trade performance are included as well as innovation. As in Chapter 4, the relationship is considered on a bilateral basis, and differences in innovation across countries are taken as one of the explanatory variables. Initially, two proxies for innovation are used, so variations in the relationship due to the choice of proxy can be observed; one is based on R&D expenditure and the other on patents taken out in the US. Chapter 5 also investigates how the relationship varies over sectors and countries. The importance of variations in the relationship either by country or by sector reflects whether it is sector characteristics, such as the level of technological opportunity in the sector, or country characteristics, such as national institutions, which most influence the role of technology. A final section uses actual counts of innovation in the UK as explanatory variables for the bilateral trade of the UK with the other countries. In addition, the ratio of innovations produced and used in each sector is used to classify the sectors into net users and net producers of innovations; the relationship between innovation and trade performance is considered separately for each group of sectors.

The third part of the book extends the analysis of the impact of technology to the international performance of firms. The last section considers the impact of innovation on trade at the level of the firm for a group of UK firms. The microeconomic perspective is taken to be particularly appropriate as technological accumulation occurs primarily at the level of the firm. The innovation history of each firm is used to characterize it as either an innovator or a non-innovator, based on a survey of innovations in the UK. The characteristics of the two groups of firms are then considered; a number of key features such as the propensity to export and the size of the firm are found to vary according to whether firms are innovators or non-innovators. Innovation is considered to give a firm a specific competitive advantage which improves its performance, including its performance on foreign markets, and leads to greater exports; in addition it may also increase the probability of a firm exporting. In order to test these propositions an empirical model of the determinants of export behaviour is set up, including both firm-specific characteristics and also characteristics of the sector in which the firm is located. Particular emphasis is placed on the innovation characteristics of both the firm and the sector. The relationship is tested both for the innovating and non-innovating firms grouped together, and for them separated, to see if the determinants of export behaviour vary over the two groups.

This microeconomic perspective on trade performance is unusual within the literature on international trade. It has been widely applied in the study of foreign direct investment by multinational companies (MNCs); firm-specific characteristics are clearly seen as one of the main causes of such investment. This part of the book aims to extend the analysis of the importance of firm-specific characteristics to explaining *export* behaviour. This is partly due to the emphasis on technology as a source of trade; innovation leads to a firm-specific advantage which can also improve a firm's performance on export markets as well as acting as an incentive to foreign direct investment. In addition, the influence of innovation can be divided into two components: that specific to the firm; and that which results from being in an innovative sector. The relative importance of these two factors can be assessed for the innovating and non-innovating firms.

Finally, Part IV presents the conclusions of the analysis. As separate conclusions are included in each chapter, the last part aims to give a broader view of the relationships between the results of all the chapters, and the implications they have for the themes discussed throughout this book. In addition, the policy implications and the limitations of the analysis are discussed.

2. The Treatment of Technology

Attempts to include technological change as a factor affecting international patterns of specialization have involved either adaptations of the neo-classical approach, or the adoption of a different approach to international trade which explicitly considers technology as of central importance. However, empirical attempts to explain patterns of specialization have frequently been characterized by an *ad hoc* approach, combining a number of different determinants of trade taken from different theoretical frameworks. This chapter delineates the principal theoretical approaches for including technology in trade models. Some readers may find the differences among theories arbitrary – for instance, between the neo-endowment and neo-technology approaches – but each has a different theoretical context which affects the way technology is perceived.

The first part of the chapter presents an overview of the Heckscher–Ohlin–Samuelson model and developments from it, as well as some empirical work inspired by it. The second section covers the so-called neo-technology theories of trade, or those theories which have given technology a central role in explaining trade patterns. Some empirical work in this area is also reviewed. Following on from the technology theories of trade, the more recent market structure approach is outlined in Section 3. Finally, the recent developments introducing endogenous technology into neo-classical models of trade leading to dynamic comparative advantage are briefly considered in Section 4.

2.1 THE HECKSCHER–OHLIN–SAMUELSON AND NEO-ENDOWMENT MODELS OF TRADE

The classical theory of international trade focused on explanations for the pattern of trade: which goods countries trade and with whom, and with the normative implications for free trade. The basis of classical theory is David Ricardo's theory of comparative advantage, which states that countries will export those goods they can produce with lowest relative costs (and therefore prices) under autarky. The contribution of this theory is that, in a two-good two-country model in which one country has an absolute advantage in producing both goods, there still exist gains from trade for both countries. Ricardo saw relative labour productivity as determining differences in costs and prices and providing the basis for comparative advantage. Neo-classical theory subsequently considered the *determinants* of comparative advantage and the resulting prices of goods and factors. The Heckscher–Ohlin–Samuelson (H–O–S) theory derives the determinants of comparative advantage in a two-good, two-factor, two-country model, predicting that a country will export those goods which use most intensively the country's more abundant factor of production. The two factors considered were capital and labour and thus the exports of a country should reflect their relative endowments of capital or labour by being either relatively capital or relatively labour intensive. In order to arrive at that prediction the theory imposes a number of limiting assumptions. The first applies to the production function, which is assumed to be static and common to all countries, ruling out technological advantage as a motivation for trade within this framework. There is also assumed to be no factor intensity reversal across countries, so that each country uses the same capital to labour ratio in the production of a certain good. The other assumptions are perfect competition and the complete mobility of factors within a country but their complete immobility between countries. Demand is also assumed to be identical across countries, with consumers maximizing an identical homothetic utility function.

The mainstream of international trade theory, then, concentrated on refining this approach (for instance the work of Vanek, generalizing the theory to more than two factors of production; for more recent extensions, see Deardorff, 1994); and the empirical testing of the theory, inspired by the work of Leontief (1953). Leontief aimed to test the factor proportions theory for the US economy, and found the famous, and at the time deeply disturbing result, that the US, assumed to be the most capital-rich country in the world, was exporting more labour-intensive goods than it was importing.[1] This became known as the Leontief paradox. The apparent lack of empirical support for the factor proportions theory led to a number of new empirical tests and refinements, and to a theoretical search for alternative explanations for the trade pattern, one strand of which was to consider technological differences as a source of trade. A more recent test of the H–O–S theory (Bowen et al. 1987) found almost no empirical support for it.

As well as considering alternative explanations for trade, the original factor proportions hypothesis was extended by subdividing the factors of production included in the model. The most important development in this field was to divide labour into skilled labour (human capital) and unskilled labour. This development was in part a reaction to the Leontief paradox for the United States; observers (including Leontief himself) assumed that the advantage in labour-intensive goods found in empirical work must reflect an advantage in *skilled* labour. Thus the original two-sector model was enlarged to include the third factor of human capital. In addition, heterogeneity within the existing category of capital was also noted, indicating the need for finer definitions of all the factors of production. This tradition, loosely named the neo-endowment approach, inspired a large number of empirical tests considering the relationship between finely defined factors of production and the export pattern of a single country (frequently the US). Courakis (1991) indicates that the composition of human capital should also be considered separately from the supply of skilled labour. Just as physical and human capital cannot be aggregated, heterogeneity within human capital should be taken account of in the assessment of a country's comparative advantage. The heterogeneity of human capital is also emphasized by Maskus et al. (1994) for US and UK trade flows.

The empirical evidence in favour of factor-proportion explanations of trade has been mixed. Many of the examinations of the relationship between factor proportions and trade have regressed an indication of the trade pattern, frequently net trade, on factors of production, initially labour and capital, for instance, Baldwin (1971) and Harkness and Kyle (1975), both for the US. With the neo-endowment models a greater number of factors were included and the factors became more closely defined. As Deardorff (1984) has pointed out, this is testing a simple commodity version of the H–O–S theory. A full examination of the theory under unbalanced trade would involve examining the difference between production and consumption (Leamer, 1980). Stern and Maskus (1981) using both regression analysis and Leontief-style input–output techniques for US trade from 1958 to 1976 found a negative relationship for physical capital in 1958 upholding the Leontief paradox, although this was not the case for 1976. The negative relationship disappeared when the natural resource industries were excluded from the model.[2] They also found skill variables to be of considerable importance in explaining the comparative advantage of the US. For the UK, Crafts and Thomas (1986) used the factor proportions framework including three factors of production, capital, unskilled labour and human capital, on historical data. They concluded that from 1870 to 1935 the UK economy was characterized by a lack of comparative advantage in skilled labour, and that UK production was labour intense with low labour productivity throughout the period.

In addition to including human capital as a factor of production, another extension of the H–O–S model was to include 'knowledge' as an endowment to the economy, which could be used as an input to the production process along with labour and capital, while maintaining the assumption of a common production function across countries. The inclusion of knowledge was closely related to the emphasis on human capital, as knowledge could be embodied in the skills of the workforce, or in capital equipment, as well as being produced through research and development (R&D) expenditure. Thus knowledge becomes another factor of production, with countries able to possess a comparative advantage in knowledge-intensive goods. However, as with capital, knowledge is a factor of production which can be produced itself, through investment in R&D and training, as can both physical and human capital through investment. As a result, these factors become endogenous in the long run, in contrast to the Ricardian factors of land and labour (ignoring mass migration movements) which are static endowments to the economy. The endogenous nature of these factors of production raises the question of the evolution of comparative advantage, and the ability of a country to create a comparative advantage.

Technology variables introduced into the factor proportions model have generally shown the importance of innovation in influencing the trade pattern of the United States. Early studies such as Gruber et al. (1967) and Keesing (1967) showed the role of R&D expenditure and scientists–engineers in the comparative advantage of the US. Stern and Maskus (1981) found technology (measured by R&D expenditure over value added) to be of considerable importance in explaining the comparative advantage of the US in 1960 and 1970 when included with a number of other factors. Following in that tradition, Sveikaukus (1983), considering US trade, assumes a single world production function, and divides inputs into many highly detailed factors. A noticeable feature of this paper is that sectors are also considered at a very detailed level, with 354 input–output industries for 1967. The paper also stands out for its detailed treatment of technology. Technology variables were included as personnel employed in research, R&D expenditure and actual data on innovations; among the latter, radical innovations were identified and included separately. The empirical model, following the Leamer (1980) methodology, shows that science and technology, more than skills or capital intensity, formed the comparative advantage of the US in 1967. In particular, the author found that the US differs from other countries in terms of R&D expenditure and the presence of major radical innovations.

As with much of the literature on international trade, there is a great deal of *ad hoc* empirical work which is not formally grounded in any single theory. As Deardorff (1984) has pointed out, this may be a weakness in the formulation of much international trade theory rather than the fault of many empirical studies. Hughes (1986), in a study of the UK, found evidence for the positive role of R&D expenditure and the negative role of foreign R&D

expenditure on UK export performance, in what could be broadly termed a neo-endowment model, as it considers the relationship between R&D and exports in terms of the relative resources within one country. However, she introduced a new element to the standard neo-endowment model by considering the potentially simultaneous relationship between exports and R&D expenditure, for which she found some evidence. For Japan, Vestal (1989) extended the neo-endowment model to consider only trade in technology, against a number of highly detailed inputs into the technological process. For trade from 1977 to 1981 he concludes that Japan was a net importer of skilled labour embodied in R&D expenditure, but a net exporter of labour connected to R&D.

The unit of analysis for empirical work on the neo-endowment theory is often the single country, frequently the US, as detailed data are needed on the various inputs such as skilled labour. In other cases a number of countries are considered, but the factor intensities of a single country are used and are taken to be the same across countries, ruling out factor intensity reversals, for example, Hufbauer (1970). Blomstrom et al. (1990), have analysed bilateral US–Swedish trade which, given the mutually high level of development of the two countries and the similarity of their natural resources, is not clearly explained by the H–O–S theory. They considered changes in the composition of trade over time, both bilaterally and for Swedish and US trade with the rest of the world and the role of technology in providing the basis for comparative advantage. Trade flows were broken down into high-medium-low-technology sectors based on the OECD (1986) classification, and US R&D intensity was used to calculate the R&D intensity of the bilateral trade flows. From both decompositions, the authors found US exports to Sweden to be more R&D intensive and in higher-technology sectors than US exports to the rest of the world. Then, using Swedish factor intensities to classify trade, they found Swedish exports to the US to be more intensive in skilled labour and R&D than Swedish exports to the rest of the world, although mostly in medium-technology sectors. As trade between the two countries has been steadily increasing since the 1970s they concluded that 'mutual technological progress may promote trade, with the new basis for specialization being the different technology levels or R&D intensities of the goods being traded, rather than initial endowments' (Blomstrom et al., 1990, p. 215). The treatment of R&D expenditure in this approach is as a factor of production, analogous to capital and labour, trade is explained in terms of relative resources, with labour separated into skilled and unskilled categories, and R&D included as an additional factor. This view of R&D expenditure as a factor of production, separates the neo-endowment approach from the neo-technology theories of trade reviewed in the following section. In the latter it is the role of innovation in creating new markets and conferring cost advantages on the innovating nation, which is emphasized.

In an attempt to consider the model for more than one country, Leamer (1974) used Bayesian techniques to assess the neo-endowments hypothesis. He examined trade flows for 28 commodity classes across 12 developed countries. In contrast to other studies he considered trade for each industry *across* countries, rather than across industries for one country, noting that the latter is an incorrect interpretation of international trade theory. He found that resource variables (capital, skills and R&D expenditure) performed poorly in explaining exports and imports, but well in explaining net exports, in particular the R&D variable. Leamer concluded that a combination of theories was required in explaining trade, and the most appropriate explanation depended on the characteristics of the sector being considered.

Overall, neo-endowment models which have included technological factors and human capital have been quite successful in explaining the net trade patterns of the US during the post-war period in which the US dominated world trade. In general, the results point to the importance of both human capital and R&D expenditure in explaining trade flows. Despite the inclusion of an increased number of factors of production, the neo-endowment approach does not tackle some of the main problems of the factor proportions theory. One problem is the inadequate treatment of technology within the theory. Technology is included as an additional factor of production, although the coexistence of inferior and superior technical capabilities and the impact this may have on relative productivity and relative growth patterns are not addressed by the neo-endowment approach. There is no account taken of the implicitly dynamic nature of technology, or the role of technology in changing the techniques available, characteristics which question the analogy between technology and labour or capital. Technological change has the capacity to be 'a chronic disturber of existing patterns of comparative advantage' (Johnson, 1975, p. 5); this aspect of technology is not adequately treated by considering technology as a static endowment to the economy.

Another weakness of the factor proportions approach is the endogeneity of the factors of production considered as determinants of trade flows. Capital, human capital and knowledge can all be accrued over time, and as a result cannot be realistically considered as fixed 'endowments' to the economy.[3] In order to tackle this problem a dynamic theory of trade is required, taking into account the accumulation of factors of production, and both the accumulation and the diffusion of technology.

2.2 TECHNOLOGY THEORIES OF TRADE

A parallel movement to the neo-endowment approach considers differences in technology as the main determinant of trade. The motivation for such theories was the explanation of the trade pattern of the US, the technologically most advanced country after the Second World War, given the apparent failure of the H–O–S model in empirical tests. Posner (1961) aimed to explain trade in manufactured goods between developed countries and abstract from other sources of trade, such as factor proportions motivated trade, and concentrate on the temporary advantage gained by a country through innovation. He found the neo-endowment approach to be a description of the relationship between exports and factors of production, but inadequate in explaining why a particular industry was located in a particular country.[4] In Posner's technology gap model of trade, a country gains a temporary advantage over its trading partners through the discovery of new products and processes. For a period of time these innovations remain unique to the innovating country until they are imitated by competitors, and the innovating country loses the advantage. However, the innovating country, by having technical superiority, can continue to innovate and maintain an advantage in a stream of new products, losing the advantage in each product, and replacing it with a new innovation.

The technology gap theory of Posner abstracted from factor endowments as a source of trade. However, some observers, such as Deardorff (1984), consider the theory to be compatible with the theory of comparative advantage. With the technology gap approach, countries can be considered to have a comparative advantage in new, and innovative products. In the Posner theory, innovations are not immediately produced in countries with a cost advantage in their production, but remain in the innovating country on account of the learning period involved in the diffusion of the innovation, and a reaction lag from the imitating country. Thus the theory predicts that countries with innovative capabilities will specialize in technology-intensive products, although because of the changing nature of the products, the goods produced in the technology-intensive country will change over time.

The technology gap theory of trade has also been formalized more recently through the work of, among others, Krugman (see 1979) and Cimoli (1988). In this model, Krugman developed a theoretical framework consisting of an innovative North which produces new products, and a non-innovative South which can produce the products only after a lag but then at a lower cost. There is only one factor of production (excluding technology), labour, which rules out any factor proportions motivated trade. Within this framework new industries must constantly emerge in the North as the older industries transfer to the South. The North's higher wages reflect the North's monopoly rent on the new technology. Such a model fits well with inter-industry trade between advanced and developing countries, but in contrast to the original Posner theory does not provide a rationale for trade between developed countries.

While neo-endowment accounts of trade have focused on single-country studies, the nature of the technology gap theory requires testing across a number of countries, as it is *differences* in technological capability which are crucial in influencing trade flows.[5] Soete (1981) considers trade flows across countries and within industries, and uses an output from the innovation process (patents) as the technology proxy, in place of the usual input of R&D expenditure. The model was estimated across the OECD countries for 40 industrial sectors, including not just manufacturing goods but also a number of resource-based sectors such as petroleum. The results show the importance of technological differences between countries in explaining trade patterns for a selection of industries. There is a great deal of heterogeneity between the different industries, implying that technological factors are of varying importance depending on the characteristics of the industry considered.

Hirsch (1965) and Vernon (1966), also sought an alternative to the H–O–S model, and they provided a dynamic theory for the location of production generally termed the product cycle theory. As in the technology gap theory, Vernon postulated a country with an advantage in producing innovations. At the early stages of production of a good, production remains in the innovating country, as a high level of skills is required to produce the good at this stage and the price of the good is high and output low. In addition, it helps to be close to the market, in order to observe consumer feedback and to give customer service. However, as the product matures and becomes more standardized, the price falls, production runs become longer and the production of the good can pass to other countries which have cost advantages in production. The innovating country then produces another new product which is located in the innovating country during the early stages of development. The theory thus involves two propositions:

- the first is that countries with a high technological capacity produce technology-intensive goods: this is consistent with the technology gap theory;
- the second is that the technology intensity of goods decreases over time as they become standardized, as in the technology gap theory products are produced in other countries after some time.

Both the technology gap and the product cycle theory thus predict that a country such as the United States will export new products. In the technology gap model it is because only the country of origin has access to the technology, while in the Vernon model it is the maturity of the product which decides its location. Both the product cycle and the technology gap approach introduce a dynamic element to international location; the dynamism refers to *products* whose characteristics change over time, and thus the requirements for their production also changes. Neither theory considers the impact of the technology on the technologically advanced *country*, what impact specialization in technologically intense products has on a country, its growth rate, and whether technologically intense and less intense countries will converge over time in terms of growth. Thus for the country, and its comparative advantage, there is no dynamic element; the dynamism refers to the product and its characteristics over time.

Walker (1979) criticized the product cycle model's emphasis on technical stability, and the standardization of production. He pointed out that Vernon's approach viewed innovation as a 'temporary dislocation', which, once over, allowed production to return to 'normality', with standardized products unaffected by innovation. As a result the product cycle gives an impression of technical stability, with products following a well-defined development pattern. As Walker points out with a number of industry case studies, it is difficult to generalize about the nature of technological change and diffusion, and only a few industries follow what could be termed a life-cycle pattern. One 'non-conformist' which he considers is the textile machinery industry, in which innovation plays a crucial role in competition, and provides a barrier to entry to new firms leading to an oligopolistic structure. As a result of learning through innovation monopoly power is maintained. The result is that the industry is characterized by a high degree of innovation and has not developed the characteristics of standardization predicted by the product cycle. The role of imitation and the diffusion of technology is given centre place in the product cycle approach, while the enduring and cumulative benefits of innovation, and the importance of monopoly power, are not considered in this 'naive' view of technological change and diffusion.

Empirical tests of the product cycle are complex because of the necessity of including an indicator for the level of standardization of each good, and considering the change in location over time. As a result, many tests have concentrated on the first static proposition that technologically intense countries produce non-standardized goods. Hufbauer (1970), with a sample of 24 countries, tried to separate the two theories, technology gap and product cycle, as explanations of trade patterns. He identified time as the crucial factor in the technology gap model, and used the 'first trade date' of a product as an indication of the age of the product. For the product cycle theory, he used the variance of the standard deviation of export unit values in each product as an indication of the standardization of the product. Hufbauer found both the first trade date of exports and the index of price variability for exports to be significantly correlated with per capita GDP, indicating that mature countries have an advantage in both new and non-standardized products. Other studies have used alternative indications for the maturity of the product;[6] high R&D expenditure is often taken as a characteristic of goods at the beginning of the life cycle. Keesing (1967) found a relationship between R&D expenditure and the United States' export performance, which he took as indicating that the US has a comparative advantage in new products.

There have also been some attempts to test the dynamic proposition of the product cycle theory. Bowen (1980) used the rate at which the price of a good declines as an indication of its level of maturity. He found little evidence for the product cycle, with the location of production not being clearly related to the price index.[7] Audretsch (1987) tested the hypothesis of whether new products are R&D intensive. He split sectors into growing, mature and declining sectors based on the trend in real sales in each sector and then looked at the relative inputs of R&D expenditure, skilled labour and capital intensity. He found that growing industries can be associated with high R&D expenditure and are intensive in skilled and unskilled labour, thus justifying the association between new products and high R&D expenditure seen in much of the literature. Aquino (1981) also found evidence that in some sectors the elasticity of trade to technology endowments falls over time. The author estimated comparative advantage in each sector on country characteristics for a selection of countries including newly industrialized countries (NICs) from 1961–74. The country attributes included a proxy for technology endowments, physical capital and scale, although there were some problems with multicollinearity between these attributes. The majority of sectors showed a decline in the elasticity of the technology variable over time, although with some exceptions.

The lack of consideration of the dynamic implications of different levels of technology for countries, and the insufficient treatment of technology by the neo-technology theories, prompted a more detailed treatment of technology and its dynamic implications. This has been supplied by the inclusion of the ideas of Schumpeter (1934, 1939, 1943) who considered innovation as the most important factor in competitiveness. He acknowledged the monopoly benefits associated with innovation, and the impact on an innovative firm's growth potential. The neo-Schumpeterian approach (Dosi et al. 1988, 1990) has incorporated two important new features into the technology gap theory of trade. The first is combining the theory with a detailed view of innovation as a microeconomic process which explains how a country can maintain a cumulative advantage in the production of technology. One of the weaknesses of the technology gap theory was the lack of explanation of *why* the innovation remained in the innovating country even in the short term, and why it was not transferred to the least-cost location (Deardorff, 1984).

The neo-Schumpeterian approach views technology as embodying specific, local, often tacit, that is, non-codifiable, and only partly appropriable knowledge. This is based on an evolutionary approach to technological change which stresses some microeconomic features of the process of innovation (Nelson and Winter, 1982). These include the *local* nature of the search for new knowledge and techniques, and the cumulative nature of technological change. Local in this case means in a technological sense, so that current innovations are influenced by past experience of innovation. As a result, most innovations are incremental improvements on existing innovations based on past experience (Rosenberg, 1982). They are frequently specific to the firm, and based on firm-level skills and learning. At the macroeconomic level these firm-specific advantages translate into a competitive advantage for the country. Each country has a particular experience of innovation, which is the aggregation of the innovation experience of its firms, as well as through complementarities between different innovations and inter-industry relationships based on the use and production of innovations. At the country level this pattern of innovation has been termed the national system of innovation of the country (Lundvall, 1992; Nelson, 1993).

At the international level, Dosi et al. (1988, 1990) stress the growth effects of specialization patterns, and the dynamic implications they may have for the economy. Most trade theorists have not considered the dynamic growth effects of a particular pattern of specialization, but rather the static redistributive gains of international specialization. The alternative view (now also shared by new growth theory) is that the pattern of specialization has dynamic implications for growth, because of differences in the innovation potential of different industries. This is based on a number of beliefs (Dosi et al., 1990): first, that international differences in rates of innovation are important determinants of both the pattern of trade and its evolution over time. Second, that the general equilibrium readjustment predicted by the neo-classical models of trade does not occur, and as a result trade can have an impact on domestic economic activity. Third, that technology is not a free good, and is not available internationally through a simple process of diffusion and technology transfer, but rather can be partly appropriated, and is accumulated at the firm and country level.

The view of technological change incorporated in this approach builds on the work of Dosi (see, for instance, 1988). Technological paradigms, or sets of technical principles, knowledge and research methods, lead to specific modes of development and technical change (technological trajectories) which are cumulative and arise from the characteristics of the technological paradigm. As a result innovation is endogenous, and the institutional environment is crucial in influencing the path of technical change. Technology has some features of an imperfect public good, the benefits from it can be appropriated to some extent, and others can be excluded from using it. Given the existence of dynamic economies of scale in the production of knowledge, a country can build up a dynamic competitive advantage in the production of new products. In addition, Dosi and Soete (1983) point out that these advantages can persist over time, causing 'virtuous' and 'vicious' cycles of development. Countries can become 'locked-in' to particular innovation and specialization patterns via their innovation history and experience (Arthur, 1989), and the nature of their institutions, thus providing a microeconomic rationale for the continuation of technological differences between countries, and the dynamic implications of specialization patterns.

The second important contribution is combining cost differences with absolute advantages in technology (see, for instance, Dosi and Soete, 1983, and Dosi et al., 1990, for a detailed description). While this approach sees technology gaps as the most important factor motivating trade, it also stresses cost advantages in explaining the trade pattern of a country, thus combining the two motivations for trade. The technology theories of trade may not be appropriate in explaining all trade flows, but rather (Johnson, 1975) can be used in conjunction with cost-based explanations of trade.

To summarize, both the technology gap and the product cycle theories predict that advanced countries will export new products. Both stress the importance of the timing of the introduction of a new technology in influencing where each good is produced, one because the diffusion of technology takes away the first-country advantage, and the other because the characteristics of the product change over time, influencing the optimal location of production. For both theories, the production of new goods (which requires research facilities) and the production of R&D-intensive goods (assumed to be goods at the early stages of maturity) will be located in countries with developed technological capabilities. Two forces act against this: one is time, which standardizes the product and increases the importance of cost considerations, and the other is the diffusion of technology, which raises the ability of foreign countries to produce new products, and imitate existing ones. The addition of neo-Schumpeterian views (Dosi et al., 1990) of technology as a microeconomic process and an important element in competition has led to a better understanding of the nature of technological advantage within the technology gap approach to trade. This has also led to a technology gap approach to growth, and differences in international patterns of growth (Fagerberg, 1987, and Soete and Verspagen, 1994).[8]

2.3 THE INTRODUCTION OF MARKET STRUCTURE

Empirical work in the 1970s again brought into question the predictive power of the factor proportions theory, but this time for different reasons. Grubel and Lloyd (1975), among others, found evidence that in the post-war period a large proportion of the tremendous increase in the volume of trade was between developed countries in the same product goods, that is, intra-industry trade. This result is contrary to the factor proportions hypothesis which predicts greater opportunities for trade between countries with different factor proportions. However, the new empirical evidence pointed to the importance of trade between countries with similar endowments and in the same product groups. While there was some discussion of the results, involving the level of aggregation, and if the trade really was in economically identical goods, most observers agreed with the general proposition that intra-industry trade had become of considerable importance. One explanation is provided by the Linder hypothesis (Linder, 1961) which, in contrast to other views of international trade, considers the role of demand in influencing trade flows. It states that similar countries will trade more with one another as they share the same tastes, so that countries with similar income levels will make products more suited for each others' markets.[9]

In order to include demand considerations and features of imperfect market structure in international economics a new theoretical framework, taken from industrial economics, was adapted. This framework explicitly included monopolistic power, economies of scale and product differentiation as factors influencing trade patterns. On the demand side, early papers such as Lancaster (1980) and Krugman (1981) hypothesized demand for a variety of goods, using utility functions in which consumers give preference to variety and want to consume a mixed set of goods. Thus product differentiation is one explanation for intra-industry trade, with horizontally differentiated goods being traded internationally, such as the cross-country demand for Citroën and Volkswagen promoting intra-industry trade between France and Germany. In addition, the existence of economies of scale causes a country to specialize in a limited number of products, while consumers have preferences for variety which leads to the simultaneous export and import of similar but differentiated products. Specialization allows low-cost production because of the exploitation of economies of scale, and trade occurs as a result of such specialization.

However, the empirical evidence on the role of economies of scale has been mixed. While the theoretical models indicate a positive relationship between economies of scale and the level of intra-industry trade, Caves (1981) found a negative relationship between economies of scale and the level of intra-industry trade for 13 industrialized countries. Greenaway and Milner (1984) also found a negative relationship for the UK between economies of scale and intra-industry trade. They assume this to be due to strong economies of scale leading to standardization of the product and thus reducing the main motivation for intra-industry trade: the desire for a variety of differentiated products. In Owen's 1983 study of the EC countries, he found a positive relationship between relative plant size (rather than firm size) and intra-industry trade between the EC countries in 1964. This relationship was limited to plant size, and thus referred to economies of scale in production rather than to economies of scale in the overall size of the firm (for instance in organization, R&D facilities, management and so on). The conflicting evidence may be partly due to a number of measurement problems which arise when including features of market structure. Both economies of scale and product differentiation are concepts that are difficult to measure, leading to the problems inherent when using proxies.[10]

Greenaway and Milner (1984) also considered R&D expenditure as a factor increasing product differentiation in their study of intra-industry trade. They separated the concept of technological differentiation, when the entire product range changes because of a technological breakthrough, from other forms of product differentiation, although as they noted in practice this separation is not possible in empirical work. They included a variable for R&D expenditure in the regression, with intra-industry trade as the dependent variable, using UK data for 1977. They hypothesized an inverted U-shaped relationship between R&D and intra-industry trade, with higher levels of R&D acting as a barrier to intra-industry trade and an incentive for specialization. However, they found little evidence for this relationship in the results.

The results from the empirical literature examining the determinants of the level of intra-industry trade between countries have been fairly consistent. They generally consider the level and difference in the development of the trading countries, per capita gross domestic product (GDP) and tariffs as explanations for intra-industry trade (see, for instance, Balassa and Bauwens, 1987). Such studies use country-level indicators to explain the proportion of intra-industry trade in total bilateral trade. The results from this empirical work appear to be quite robust. One result is that the greater the difference in per capita incomes, the lower is the share of intra-industry trade between two countries. This may be due to supply-side considerations, such as differences in the labour/capital ratio, or due to taste differences as in the Linder hypothesis, see, for instance, Lundberg (1988). There appears to be a positive relationship between the level of average per capita income and intra-industry trade, interpreted as the rise in the demand for differentiated goods as incomes increase. The volume of intra-industry trade seems to fall in the presence of tariff barriers (Balassa, 1986).

Overall, the main contribution of this approach has been the formalization of new models of international trade, explicitly incorporating many of the features ruled out in the neo-classical model. Helpman (1981) combined the two approaches into one model, in which there is one standardized product (food) which has no economies of scale and cannot be differentiated, and a continuum of differentiated manufacturing products each with an identical production function characterized by economies of scale. Each country produces different varieties of the non-standardized product and then trades them so there is intra-industry trade. However, the net trade pattern between the countries is still explained by the H–O–S theory, with the more labour-abundant country producing the more labour-intensive product. This paper provided an important synthesis, incorporating the new market structure explanations for trade into the neo-classical approach, so that despite what seemed important empirical evidence against the factor proportions model, the latter is still given some role in explaining trade flows. However, the important assumption of identical technologies across countries is maintained, leading to identical costs, and in addition consumers have identical utility functions. It is only in terms of population and stocks of capital that the countries can differ, leading to endowment differences as a source of trade: the important issue of differences in technology is not addressed by this model.

In the spirit of the 1981 Helpman model, Bergstrand (1990) attempted to separate the influences of supply considerations (the capital to labour ratio) from demand considerations (the size and similarity of demand). This required separating the effects of differences between national incomes and the level of national income and per capita income, from differences between, and the level of, capital to labour endowment ratios. This was necessary because of the debate over the interpretation of many of the empirical results which had excluded the capital to labour ratio. Because of its exclusion, the explanatory variables as well as reflecting demand considerations, could also have been acting as a proxy for supply factors, omitted from the model. The results from the Bergstrand paper, using data for 14 major industrialized countries in 1976, confirmed that intra-industry trade falls as a percentage of bilateral trade given increases in the differences between countries' GDP and GDP per capita, and rises with the levels of GDP and GDP per capita. The author concludes that this is due both to supply reasons (H–O–S) and to demand reasons (the Linder hypothesis), simultaneously. In another attempt to test the Helpman model, Balassa and Bauwens (1988) found that factor intensities explained the pattern of inter-industry trade, that is, net trade, but that a combination of country and sector characteristics were important in explaining intra-industry trade.

Within this approach, some attention has also been given to the strategic relationship between monopolistic firms in different countries, and the role that R&D has in monopolistic behaviour. Brander and Spencer (1983) have considered the strategic role of R&D expenditure in capturing new markets. In this model, *which* good is produced and traded is now of primary importance to the trading country, as in some sectors there is the possibility of exploiting monopoly rents. As Brander and Spencer point out: 'it is to the advantage of a country to "capture" a larger operating share of the production of imperfectly competitive rent earning industries operating in the international markets' (p. 708). Thus country-level R&D is rivalrous, giving an explanation for the existence of national subsidies for R&D expenditure. In this vein, Audretsch and Yamawaki (1987) considered the role of strategic R&D expenditure in US–Japanese bilateral trade in the 1970s. They found that R&D expenditure generally promoted Japanese trade although it was more effective in some cases than in others: expenditure on R&D could improve a country's market share abroad and as a result could be used as a strategic weapon in trade.

An alternative strand of theory, emphasizing market and firm structure, has concentrated on international capital mobility through multinational companies (MNCs). Clearly the presence and importance of MNCs questions the neo-classical assumption of internationally immobile factors of production, when such firms can move production internationally maintaining firm-specific advantages such as knowledge, management practices, capital and skills. The presence of firm-specific benefits as a motivation for foreign direct investment has led to the explicit consideration of the role of technological capabilities in promoting foreign direct investment. Cantwell (1989) considers the relationship between firm-specific advantages and comparative advantage in influencing the international pattern of trade and production. The dynamic framework of this approach builds on the product cycle theory and evolutionary theories of technological accumulation. Technology is characterized as both firm specific and cumulative and thus becomes an advantage for a particular firm, although it is influenced by the location both of the parent company and of the subsidiaries.

In summary, the market structure approach introduced powerful new theoretical models which have subsequently been integrated into the factor proportions tradition. The empirical evidence for specific features of imperfect competition, such as economies of scale, has been mixed. Nevertheless, some general results about the proportion of intra-industry trade between countries have been obtained. The treatment of technology in the market structure approach has taken two forms. The first is as a factor adding to product differentiation, and thus the technology intensity of products can be used as a proxy for their heterogeneity. Second, the strategic nature of technology has been considered by Brander and Spencer (1983), who model technology as conferring a strategic advantage to a country by capturing the monopoly rents from innovation.

2.4 DYNAMIC COMPARATIVE ADVANTAGE

The view of technology as a strategic tool which can be manipulated to gain a trade advantage, was the precursor to a dynamic theory of comparative advantage considering technology as endogenous. The neo-classical tradition in international economics was always a static tradition, considering endowments as given and irreversible. It was left to the technology theories of trade, in particular the product cycle approach, to consider the dynamic nature of comparative advantage especially for new products. The development of new techniques has led to the treatment of innovation as an endogenous factor, initially in the context of growth theory (for instance, Romer, 1990) but the implications were also applied to trade theory leading to models in which comparative advantage itself is endogenous and can be created over time, and the export specialization of a country can affect its growth rate.

This is a heterogeneous literature with results varying according to individual models.[11] In the model by Grossman and Helpman (1990), comparative advantage is defined as cross-country differences in efficiency at R&D versus manufacturing. The economy is in three sectors with an R&D sector creating new designs for products subsequently produced in the intermediate goods sector where goods are non-tradable, and a final goods sector where perfect competition prevails at the firm level, and there are dynamic economies of scale at the industry level. This is a one-factor model with the factor being termed labour (excluding technology), but the productivity of it varies internationally giving rise to comparative advantage. The main outcome of the model is that comparative advantage can be *acquired* through experience in research which raises relative productivity at R&D, and increases the growth rate of the country through increasing returns to scale. By specializing in the R&D sector a country can achieve a higher growth rate: thus export specialization has important long-run consequences. In Krugman (1987) the outcome is the same, although the mechanism of the model is different. Learning by doing is included so that knowledge is accumulated over time and comparative advantage is based on differences in learning. Experience in production is of critical importance as learning can occur only through production: as a result, changes in relative productivity act to lock countries into their original pattern of production, making export specialization static over time. The only force acting against this accumulated learning benefit is the diffusion of technology to foreign producers. Initial conditions and history are important in creating comparative advantage over time via the dynamics of learning.

The inclusion of learning, and the cumulative and endogenous nature of technology leading to endogenous comparative advantage based on differences in technology, makes dynamic models of comparative advantage closer to the neo-Schumpeterian models outlined in Section 2. Technology, and the accumulation of technology (or 'knowledge') is allowed to vary internationally, so the neo-classical assumption of a common production function across countries has been dropped. As a result, differences in technology become one of the main explanations of comparative advantage. However, despite this notion of the creation of comparative advantage, in their review of the 'new' growth theory and its relation to international trade Grossman and Helpman (1990, p. 86) state that: 'familiar notions of comparative advantage may determine to what extent particular countries are led to specialise in the creation of knowledge and in the production of goods that make intensive use of human capital and new technologies', that is, causality still runs from comparative advantage to the accumulation of technology. A country does not have an absolute advantage because of technology, as in the neo-Schumpeterian approach. In the same article the authors also stress the importance of spillovers between countries, due to cheap and rapid communication. This is in direct contrast to the microeconomic view of technology as cumulative and path dependent, emphasized by the evolutionary perspective, which while acknowledging the role of spillovers, and the diffusion of technology, also highlights the mechanisms by which countries build up cumulative experience in innovation.

Much of both the new growth and new trade theory assumes that there are outputs from the innovation process. One part of the output from research and development is appropriable, and this gives the financial incentive to producers to invest in innovation. The other part goes into a 'pool' of knowledge, which can also be accessed by the firms' competitors. Thus investment in innovation responds to market pressures, but innovation also has certain public good features. It would appear to be the balance between these two elements which characterizes the two different approaches. The neo-Schumpeterian approach emphasizes the firm-specific element of innovation, while the 'new' international trade theory stresses spillovers and the public good aspects of innovation.

2.5 SUMMARY

The development of international trade theory can be separated into three main strands. The first is the neo-classical approach, setting comparative advantage in a general equilibrium framework, giving rise to the factor proportions explanation for observed trade patterns. This tradition has seen a widening of the definition of factors of production, in the neo-endowment model, and has ultimately taken account of the dynamic implications of endogenous technology.

The second strand of trade theory is made up of market structure models adapted from industrial economics. These incorporate features of imperfect competition, such as monopoly power and economies of scale, into international economics. The ensuing synthesis between market structure models and the Heckscher–Ohlin model suggests that they are not necessarily contradictory, and can be mutually complementary. As far as the innovation process is concerned, both approaches suffer from an incomplete treatment of innovation, and the dynamic role it plays in economic growth.

The third strand contains those theories which have not formed part of the neo-classical tradition and have not been absorbed into the mainstream of trade theory.[12] The neo-technology theories date from the 1960s, and as early as 1967 Gruber et al. (1967, p. 22) stated that 'all roads lead to a link between export performance and R&D'. Nevertheless, the neo-technology theories, despite placing technology at centre stage, suffer from the same basic weakness as attempts to incorporate technology into the neo-classical model. Some key characteristics of technology – such as the dynamic implications from monopoly power and technological change – have been consistently neglected. The specialization pattern of a particular economy was still considered to be neutral in terms of domestic growth.

To overcome some of these problems, a Schumpeterian view of innovation has been incorporated into neo-technology theories of trade. On the one hand, the technology gap hypothesis has been combined with an evolutionary view of technology, considering the dynamic implications of technology gaps on growth and specialization patterns. On the other hand, the firm-specific nature of technology and the monopoly power associated with successful innovation have been used to explain foreign direct investment (Cantwell, 1989), as firms strive to maintain their technological advantage within the firm. Both these developments question the limited dynamics of the technology gap and product cycle theories. Technology gaps may not be temporary, and the advantages of innovation may not diffuse cyclically to other countries and producers; this does not alter the static proposition that in a cross-section we would expect to find a relationship between differences in technology between countries and relative trade performance.

NOTES

1. Leamer (1980) has shown that in fact Leontief's test was not a correct test of the factor proportions theory. Nevertheless, other tests covering the same period (for example, Stern and Maskus, 1981) also find that the Leontief 'paradox' holds, with the US exporting relatively labour-intensive goods, although the paradox does not appear to hold for later periods. Wood (1994) argues that most tests of the H–O–S model are mis-specified, and when correctly specified the model can still be 'illuminating'. This is a subject for a book in itself, and will not be dealt with here.
2. Another criticism of the two-factor approach is that natural resources are not included; this is a potential explanation for the Leontief paradox.
3. As Fagerberg (1994b p. 8) puts it 'to label something "endowment" – when it clearly reflects conscious human behaviour – does not constitute much of an explanation'.
4. As Posner ironically points out, to say that watch making is located in Switzerland is because of endowments of labour skilled in watch making is not an explanation.
5. There have also been a number of industry case studies, such as Freeman (1963) for the plastics industry. He found that technological progress could give leadership in production by 10 to 15 years through a combination of patent protection and secrecy.
6. See Wells (1972) for some early studies on the product cycle model.
7. This could be because of weaknesses in the price index used.
8. For a review of the literature on technology and growth, see Fagerberg (1994b).
9. Note that this is in complete contradiction to the prediction of the H–O–S model that countries with different factor endowments will trade more with each other.
10. See, for instance, Greenaway (1983) for a discussion of the measurement of product differentiation.
11. Verspagen (1993) gives a comprehensive overview of the new growth theory and its relationship to evolutionary theory.
12. See Bensel and Elmslie (1992) for an appraisal of the methodology of international trade theory.

3. Measuring the Impact of Technology

This chapter aims to consider the empirical work which has focused on the impact of innovation patterns on trade performance. As much of the empirical work is not clearly linked to a specific theory of trade, the literature is organized into three sections which correspond to important features of the empirical work. The first is whether the empirical model considered is dynamic or static. A dynamic model is defined as one which aims to explain the evolution in trade patterns of particular countries over time, rather than attempting to explain the static trade specialization at any one point in time. The majority of international trade theories has concentrated on explaining static specialization patterns. Although studies frequently use lagged independent innovation variables to account for the delay in the impact of innovation on trade performance, they do not specifically examine the evolution of trade patterns over time. However, there have been a number of recent studies considering the dynamic implications of technology on trade using time-series data.

The second feature of the empirical literature is whether the empirical model has been tested for a single country across sectors, or for each sector across countries. The choice of a country-specific or commodity-specific test reflects the theoretical context of the model. In order to test the technology gap theory of trade, technology differences between countries are required and the ideal test is for each sector across countries: single-country tests contrast the trade specialization pattern of a country with its technological specialization pattern.

The third feature of empirical models is the choice of innovation proxy. As few direct measures of innovation are available, a proxy is normally used which may be either an input into the innovation process, such as R&D expenditure, or an output such as patent counts. As each proxy generally captures only certain aspects of the innovation process, the choice of proxy is an important element of empirical tests, and can influence the results.

3.1 DYNAMIC OR STATIC MODELS?

The first issue is whether the empirical model considered is dynamic or static. Most of the work fits into the second category – testing static models – as most theoretical models consider equilibrium relationships between the determinants of trade and trade patterns. For the neo-technology theories of trade, this means taking a 'snapshot' of the trade patterns between countries (frequently between pairs of countries) and relating them to differences in technological capabilities between the countries.

Many static tests of the technology gap theory have considered correlations between a technology index and trade performance, and abstracted from other sources of trade. This has been done both for sectors across countries (Pavitt and Soete, 1980, and Soete, 1987) and across sectors for countries (Amendola et al., 1991, and van Hulst et al., 1991). For the former tests, OECD countries were used with data disaggregated to 40 sectors. Exports for 1977 were correlated with patents taken out in the US, simultaneously in 1977 and cumulatively from 1963 to 1977. Both the export and the patent variables were scaled by the country's population in order to account for country size. In this sector-level study, patents were found to be significantly related to trade performance in 19 of the 40 sectors, mostly the machinery sectors and the majority of high-technology sectors (with the exceptions of aircraft and office equipment).

Other tests have included additional factors as explanatory variables such as Soete's 1981 test of the technology gap model, which found that relative technological performance was an important factor in the trade performance of OECD countries. A number of dependent variables were used including the share of exports, revealed comparative advantage[1] and the export to import ratio: the best results were obtained with the share of exports as the dependent variable. This analysis is updated in both Dosi and Soete (1983) and Dosi et al. (1990); the results confirm an important role for technology. Dosi et al. (1990) set out two empirical tests of parts of the neo-Schumpeterian approach outlined in the book. Both models took absolute advantages as the basis for trade, using export shares and exports per capita as the dependent variables. The results confirm the important role of technology in explaining trade performance.

There are a number of recent attempts to consider the impact of technology on the growth of trade over time, and the long-term effects which innovation may have on export performance. As Amendola et al. (1993) have pointed out, either mis-specifying or ignoring the dynamics of the relationship may lead to biased results, and could be one explanation for seemingly paradoxical results such as those found by Kaldor (1978).[2] As a result, Amendola et al.

test a dynamic model of the determinants of trade, estimating both the short- and long-run effects of the explanatory variables, including technology, on export market shares. By including an autoregressive dependent variable in the specification, the importance of past trade performance on present trade performance ('success breeds success') can be partly accounted for. The authors use patents as the innovation variable, with time-series data, although the data are not disaggregated by sector. The results show the significant long-run effects of the patent and investment variables (both taken as reflecting technological capability) while the labour-cost variable had only a short-term effect on exports. Amendola et al. conclude that innovation and investment in the capital stock can shape the long-term trade performance of a country.

Fagerberg (1988) also considers a dynamic model of international competitiveness using country-level data. He develops and estimates a complete model of international competitiveness, which relates growth in market shares to innovation and price competition, taking capacity considerations into account. The model is dynamic in the sense that it is *growth* in export market share (on the world market), along with growth in import share and growth in GDP, which are considered as the dependent variables. Both the relative level of technology and the growth of a country's technological competitiveness were included as explanatory variables. The former (the technology gap) was found to be negatively significant and the latter (growth in domestic technological competitiveness) positively significant. Fagerberg concludes that both capacity and technology have important medium-term and long-term implications for growth in market shares and GDP, while cost considerations play less of a role than has formerly been thought.

Dosi et al. (1990) also test the dynamic implications of changes in technology for changes both in the growth of exports and in the trade balance for the period 1964 to 1980. Because of data limitations the analysis is across the OECD countries for the whole of manufacturing industry, rather than on the disaggregated sector level of the static tests. The technological indicators, which are growth in US patents and growth in labour productivity, both perform well in explaining changes in exports over the whole period, but not as well for the period of the 1970s: the authors conclude that this may be due to exchange rate variations in that period. Verspagen (1993) extended these tests for a large selection of countries, including many newly industrialized countries (NICs) as well as the OECD countries. The results confirmed that technology is a key variable in explaining market shares, especially for high-technology and medium-technology sectors. The author also estimated a dynamic evolutionary model which included two components: one was the last period market share; and the other was a term for country j's competitiveness relative to average competitiveness and multiplied by the last period market share. In this model the innovation variable was significant only in the case of a few sectors, and then frequently with a negative sign. In addition, the wage rate was significant in most cases, in contrast to the static model in which little role was found for the wage-rate variable. The results for the dynamic model appear to contradict those for the static model: some sectors have positive patent coefficients for the static model, and negative for the dynamic. The author gives a number of reasons for this negative relationship. The sample includes many NICs, which have improved their market share through imitation, rather than innovation, and have often either evaded or violated international patent restrictions. As a result, patents may not be the best proxy in capturing technological competitiveness, as they fail to capture the diffusion of technology. In addition, the patent variable cannot capture the role of MNCs in producing abroad, as their patents will refer to the home country rather than the country where production is located.

Other papers, such as Cotsomitis et al. (1991), have also noted the need for a dynamic model to test the impact of technology on trade performance. The authors found technology gaps, proxied with a relative patent stock variable, to be significant and with the expected sign in only 11 per cent of the cases they considered. However, there are a number of inconsistencies in the test which are worth considering. First there is the choice of countries: 14 OECD countries excluding the US (surely one of the most important sources of technology gaps in the OECD) and the UK, and including many of the smaller OECD countries.[3] They have also used a narrow selection of sectors, which affects the results as the relationship has been found to vary considerably on a sector basis. In addition, the authors did not take some of the precautions necessary when using time series, for example, they did not test for stationarity, and they did not investigate the most appropriate lag structure for the technology variable. The latter may be one explanation for the high number of significant coefficients for the technology variable with perverse signs in their results.

Magnier and Toujas-Bernate (1994) have tested a dynamic model of the impact of price and non-price factors on the export market shares of countries in particular sectors. They took new international economics as their theoretical framework, with its implications for the strategic value of technology in improving a country's trade performance. They included innovation (relative R&D expenditures) and capacity (relative fixed investment) as indicators of non-price factors in competitiveness, along with an indication of relative prices. As they expected, they found price effects to be relatively weak and non-price effects to have an important influence on trade performance in the long run. They used a partial adjustment specification with both country-specific and industry-specific effects, a less restricted model than others using either country-level data in a dynamic model, or a cross-section specification.

In the tradition of this error-correction model, Amable and Verspagen (1995) estimate a similar model, but they allow the speed of adjustment to the long-run target market share to vary over countries. Their results confirm the importance of innovation in the majority of sectors considered. Verspagen and Wakelin (1997a) also used an error-correction mechanism in their model, although they considered the data pooled over two periods, the 1970s and the 1980s, and not as time series. They substituted two different technology variables, relative R&D expenditures and patents, and found that the results changed for a number of the sectors considered. The results confirmed the importance of technology, and the degree of variation over sectors.

All three of the papers cited above using an error-correction mechanism allow some degree of variation for the relationship estimated over sectors and countries, while the two papers by Fagerberg (1988) and Amendola et al. (1993) consider the relationship across time and countries, and allow country-specific effects. Greenhalgh (1990) and Greenhalgh et al. (1992, 1994) consider a dynamic model of the influence of price and non-price effects on trade performance over time, and by sector, for a single country, the UK. In Greenhalgh (1990), non-price effects were included using data on the number of strikes, a proxy for the reliability of supply, and the number of innovations which occurred in the UK, taken as a proxy for product quality. The model estimated includes domestic income (world income was dropped as it was highly correlated with domestic income) and relative prices for exports and imports, as well as the number of strikes and innovations. The model is estimated from 1954 to 1981 and for 33 trading sectors, including non-manufacturing sectors. First, the order of integration of the variables was investigated. As the variables appeared to be cointegrated, cointegrating-level equations were estimated by OLS in order to look at the long-run impact of the determinants on trade performance. In addition, a second error-correction mechanism model was estimated to investigate the short-run dynamics, and to provide alternative estimates of the long-run elasticities. A number of innovation variables were experimented with and the best fit model was chosen. The results showed important long-run effects of innovation on trade performance in half of the industries considered. However, a number of core innovating industries, such as the engineering sectors, did not appear to have their trade performance benefit as a result of innovation within the sector. Greenhalgh concludes that 'there are beneficial externalities flowing from the core innovators, who nevertheless remain vulnerable to external competition' (Greenhalgh, 1990, p. 117).

Greenhalgh et al. (1994) investigate the impact of innovation on the price and volume of exports from the UK, using the same methodology. They find evidence for the positive role of innovation on trade performance and the low price elasticities of many sectors, which they take to indicate the existence of imperfect competition in those sectors. However, they did note that some high-technology sectors experienced a high degree of price competition, making them vulnerable to cost rises and changes in the exchange rate. They found no general price effects from innovation, but that both price rises and reductions were possible outcomes, although they did find a general improvement in trade volumes and the balance of trade as a result of innovation.

To summarize, most empirical studies are undertaken in a static framework; and examine the relationship between a technology indicator and relative trade performance, either in the form of correlations or with a multivariate analysis. These results have found considerable evidence for the role of technology in affecting trade performance, for developed countries. More recently there have been attempts to test dynamic versions of the model. The dynamic models confirm the importance of technology and technological differences in trade performance, and in particular the long-run impact that technology can have on trade performance, relative to the more short-run dynamics of other factors, such as relative labour costs. Overall, the literature points to the importance of non-price factors, such as quality and innovation, in influencing the trade performance of developed countries.

3.2 COUNTRY OR COMMODITY SPECIFIC?

The second characteristic of the literature is whether the models are estimated across countries for a single industry, or across industries for a single country.[4] In the case of time-series models, the additional dimension of time allows separate estimates to be made for single sectors and countries. Table 3.1 shows the empirical studies classified into two groups – static and dynamic – and according to whether they were made for each sector across countries (column 2), for each country across sectors (column 3) or over time (column 4). None of the dynamic models is estimated over sectors, but some are estimated over both time and countries (column 3). Typically, neo-endowment models have considered the impact of technology on the trade performance of a single country, and have taken sector variations in endowments of technology as one of the determinants of the country's sectoral pattern of trade performance. This is consistent with most of the studies, which run regressions on a cross-section of industries for particular countries in an attempt to explain the trade pattern of a given country.

Table 3.1 A classification of the literature

	Over countries	Over sectors	Over time
Levels	Pavitt and Soete (1980) Dosi and Soete (1983) Soete (1981, 1987) Antonelli (1986) Dosi et al. (1990) Peretto (1990) Cotsomitis et al. (1991*) Daniels (1993) Fagerberg (1994b)	Gruber and Vernon (1970) Momigliano and Siniscalco (1984) Hughes (1986) Amendola et al. (1991) van Hulst et al. (1991) Buxton et al. (1991)	Greenhalgh (1990) Greenhalgh et al. (1992) Greenhalgh et al. (1994) Cotsomitis et al. (1991)
	Over countries	Over time and countries	Over time
Change	Magnier and Toujas-Bernate (1994) Amable and Verspagen (1995) Verspagen (1993) Verspagen and Wakelin (1997a) Fagerberg (1994b)	Fagerberg (1988) Amendola et al. (1993) Dosi et al. (1990)	Greenhalgh (1990) Greenhalgh et al. (1992) Greenhalgh et al. (1994)

Note: * This is also over time.

Likewise, in his test of the technology gap theory of trade, Soete (1981) stressed that it is *inter-country* differences in technology which are one of the main motivations for trade flows between countries. Thus a single-country cross-industry analysis of the impact of technology on trade does not provide the correct framework for examining the neo-technology theories of trade, as they take account only of the distribution of innovative resources within a country (typically using R&D expenditure as a proxy for innovativeness) and not the relative innovativeness of different countries within a sector. An inter-country framework for analysis is also suggested by the 'new' international trade theory, which emphasizes the strategic and rivalrous nature of investment in innovation (see, for instance, Brander and Spencer, 1983), and how differences in commitment to innovation can affect different countries' trade performances.

The choice between cross-country and cross-sector models also mirrors a more fundamental debate concerning the determinants of trade performance. The inter-country studies concentrate on *absolute* advantages in innovation as the motivating factor for trade, while inter-industry studies consider technology as another endowment to be considered in assessing the *comparative* advantage of a country and its resulting trade pattern. It is the absolute nature of the trade advantage in the technology gap model which Cotsomitis et al. (1991) blame for its poor performance in their empirical test, stating that not considering the advantage of the country in all products *vis-à-vis* the partner country is a serious theoretical weakness of the technology gap theory of trade. The issue of absolute or comparative advantage strongly influences the choice of dependent variable. While most of the studies already considered in the earlier section used some indication of absolute advantages in trade (the export to import ratio, or country j's share of OECD exports), many single-country studies use revealed comparative advantage as an indication of the inter-sectoral export specialization pattern of a single country.

Alternatively, a sector-specific cross-country model can use country-level capabilities to explain sectoral trade performance. Fagerberg (1994b) considered export specialization (using a revealed comparative advantage index) for each sector in each country as the dependent variable, but used country characteristics as the explanatory variables. The most important country characteristics considered were technology (both R&D and foreign patents), wages, and scale (population), and the results were used to assess the importance of these three factors for each sector, and the interdependencies between them. Out of the 28 sectors considered, the 20 sectors with significant results showed that different combinations of the explanatory factors were important, although out of the three factors technology was the most important overall. Considering both the static and dynamic models, the author concludes that 'technology is the only factor that has sufficient explanatory power to explain both the statics and dynamics of the model' (Fagerberg, 1994b, p. 11).

Daniels (1993) also considered the technology gap relationship using the framework set out in Dosi et al. (1990). His empirical analysis varied from earlier studies in two major ways. The first is the inclusion of a large (52) and mixed group of countries, including NICs such as Brazil, Mexico and Korea. Because of this broad choice of countries the author took trade performance in one large technology-intensive sector, chosen on the basis of sectoral R&D intensity, so that the test was intra-sectoral and across countries but at a more aggregate level than other studies. Technological activity was proxied both with patents and with R&D expenditure, and the number of scientists and engineers was included as a measure of human capital: the former performed very well, and had a positive relationship with trade performance in all cases. The human capital variable had a more mixed performance. Thus the importance of technology as a motivating factor in trade does not appear to be limited just to trade between OECD countries, but to include a wider and more heterogeneous group of trade flows.

Amendola et al. (1991) consider the evolution of trade and technology specialization using revealed comparative advantage indices for trade, and analogous indicators for technological specialization. The model was estimated for each country across sectors. Summarizing the results of the correlations, the authors concluded that countries could be roughly considered in three groups. The first is made up of world trade leaders (Germany and Japan) with a generally positive and significant relationship between trade and technology specialization; the second group comprises intermediate-sized countries (such as France and the UK) which have a significant relationship only in some periods; and the third consists of small countries which have significant relationships (for example, Sweden and the Netherlands). This result confirms other analyses (Soete, 1987; Fagerberg, 1988) which have found that the trade performance of small countries is particularly influenced by their pattern of innovation.

While the above studies took a number of countries, there are also a number of studies which have concentrated on the export pattern of one country, for instance Hughes (1986) for the UK, Momigliano and Siniscalco (1984) for Italy, and Gruber and Vernon (1970) for the US. Such studies generally fit the neo-endowment framework, considering technology as an endowment and relating it to inter-sectoral trade performance. The results of country-level studies are very mixed: Hughes finds evidence that innovation plays a role in exports for the UK, while the results for Italy imply a negative relationship between technology intensity and exports, but a positive and significant one for skilled labour.

Buxton et al. (1991) also examined the impact of R&D expenditure on the trade performance of a single country (the UK), but included variables for prices, income and R&D expenditure of 'the rest of the world'. For the R&D variable this was for four of the UK's major trading partners. A positive relationship was found for the UK technology variable, both on exports and the trade balance, and a negative one for the world technology variable. The authors emphasized the importance of *relative* R&D for trade performance, and the need to assess a country's technological capital over time, making the technology stock variable more appropriate than a flow variable such as R&D expenditure.

Recent developments using panel data methods have also been applied to the impact of technology on trade (Peretto, 1990) and provide one solution to the problem of assuming a constant relationship either across countries or across sectors. Peretto included country and sector fixed effects in the pooled model, both separately and together. He found evidence of strong sector effects, and concluded that economic structure is linked in a sector-specific way to competitiveness. In comparison, he found evidence of only weak country effects, although the model with both effects included also performed well.

While most of the papers reviewed in this chapter are concerned with the impact of technology on trade and growth patterns, there is a body of literature concerned with explaining the development of a country's technology profile. This literature considers the development of *national systems of innovation*, and the impact that domestic economic structure has on technology (see, for instance, Lundvall, 1992). The structure of the domestic economy, its sectoral specialization and linkages between sectors influence the processes of learning and innovation. The subsequent technology profile affects export specialization and thus has a large overlap with the literature considering the role of technology in influencing trade patterns. Country-specific patterns of innovation, and the factors which created them, such as institutions, remain important determinants of trade specialization. There has been considerable recent interest in analysing national innovation systems (see, for instance, Nelson, 1993) and their role in domestic economic growth patterns. Most studies point to the heterogeneity of patterns of innovation specialization among developed countries (for example, Guerrieri, 1991, for more than eighty countries), and even among the EC countries (Archibugi and Pianta, 1992, 1993), and the static nature of trade specialization patterns over time (Dalum, 1992), although there are also some dissenting views (Soete and Verspagen, 1994).

Dalum has considered, at a highly aggregate level, the specialization patterns of the OECD countries, and their development pattern over time. He concludes that 'an internationally specialized engineering sector has been a major, though not sufficient, condition for the successful long term economic strength of the OECD countries' (Dalum, 1992, p. 207). Fagerberg (1992) in the same volume, tests the home market hypothesis, which is part of the mechanism for the impact of domestic structure on export specialization. The hypothesis, taken from Linder (1961), suggests that co-operation between users and producers of technology tends to be localized. As a result, demand in the home market for certain products and processes can be more easily supplied by domestic producers, who are better informed about the home market, and thus respond to the demand with innovations which are tested in the home market. These domestic user–producer relationships have a subsequent impact on domestic export specialization. For 14 out of the 23 sectors the hypothesis of no home market effect was rejected. Fagerberg concluded that the home market hypothesis is important for some products, particularly in those sectors in which innovation plays a significant role, but remains a partial explanation for trade specialization.

To summarize, an appropriate test for the technology gap theory of trade is for each sector across countries, as it is relative innovation that is of interest (Hufbauer, 1970; Soete, 1981). For many of the dynamic models, sectoral disaggregation was not possible because of data limitations, and as a result many of these models are estimated either over time for single countries, or across countries and time. In some cases when single-country models were estimated relative technology variables were used, with the technological capabilities of the home country being assessed relative to their competitors. Models estimated over sectors for countries consider the impact of the domestic technology profile on domestic trade performance, and as a result cannot be considered as tests of the technology gap theory.

3.3 THE CHOICE OF INNOVATION PROXY

The third major issue is the choice of proxy used for innovation in the model. As there are few direct measures of innovations, and those that do exist generally cover only one country, an alternative measurable aspect of the innovation process needs to be used as a proxy. The main choice has been between using an input to the innovation process, such as R&D expenditure or the number of scientists and engineers employed in research departments, or an output from innovation such as patents. As Table 3.2 shows, most of the papers considering the relationship between trade and technology have used one of these two proxies, although the exact treatment of the proxy may vary between them.

As the earlier discussion pointed out, *relative* technological capabilities are required in order to test the technology gap model. Patents taken out domestically are not appropriate, because institutional differences between countries make it impossible to compare domestic patent counts, and as a result foreign patents have been used for all the patent proxies. Generally,

Table 3.2 A classification of innovation proxies in the literature

Patent based	R&D expenditure based	Innovation counts	Both proxies
Pavitt and Soete (1980)	Hughes (1986)	Greenhalgh (1990)	Fagerberg (1988)
Soete (1981, 1987)	Magnier and Toujas-Bernate (1994)	Greenhalgh et al. (1992)	Peretto (1990)
Dosi and Soete (1983)	Verspagen and Wakelin (1997a)	Greenhalgh et al. (1994)	Aquino (1981)
Dosi et al. (1990)	Buxton et al. (1991**)		
Cotsomitis et al (1991*)	Daniels (1993)		
van Hulst et al. (1991)	Peretto (1990***)		
Amendola et al. (1991)	Momigliano and Siniscalco (1984)		
Amendola et al. (1993)	Fagerberg (1994b)		
Amable and Verspagen (1995)			
Verspagen and Wakelin (1997a)			
Daniels (1993)			
Verspagen (1993****)			
Fagerberg (1994b)			

Notes
*   This is a patent stock variable, weighted according to the age of the patent, with more recent
       patents given a greater weight.
**   This is an R&D stock variable, using two depreciation rates.
***   Includes also cumulative value added as an indication of 'learning'.
**** Also includes labour productivity as an indicator of technical change.

patents taken out in the US are considered (Fagerberg, 1988, uses all foreign patents), as this is the largest international market; some correction is needed for the US, which will clearly have a domestic bias.

Soete (1981, 1987) championed the use of a measure of the output from the innovation process, such as patent statistics, in testing the technology gap model, because of the emphasis on new products and product innovation in the theory which explicitly calls for an output rather than an input measure. Patents also capture the 'monopoly-time element' (Soete, 1981) emphasized in the theory, as they can be used to protect a temporary monopoly in a new product or process.[5] Following the Soete tradition, patents have been widely used in the recent literature on trade and technology (Cotsomitis et al., 1991; Amendola et al., 1993; Amable and Verspagen, 1995). An alternative proxy for the technology gap model was suggested by Hufbauer (1970), who considered the first trade date as a proxy for the age of the product, in order to capture the element of time in the technology gap model.

The incompatibility of R&D data across countries has been one of the problems which has favoured the use of patents in cross-country studies, and has led to the use of the OECD countries for which better-quality data are available. This problem does not arise for single-country studies: detailed disaggregate R&D data are generally available for single countries and are widely used (Hughes, 1986; Momigliano and Siniscalco, 1984). When using R&D data there is also the issue of whether or not to include military expenditure on R&D. For a number of countries (for instance the US, the UK and France) military expenditure is a significant proportion of domestic R&D, and certainly in the case of the US and the UK has dominated the domestic research agenda in some sectors. However, military R&D may have lower spillovers to the rest of the economy than other forms of research, for reasons such as secrecy and lack of market criteria in the research (see Kaldor et al., 1986, for the UK). This may decrease its value as part of a country's technological capabilities, although in some key sectors such as aerospace it may be important in explaining trade performance, and the presence of high military expenditure can influence the national innovation profile of a country, as seems to have been the case for the UK (Walker, 1993).

Both patent and R&D proxies capture different aspects of innovation which may vary systematically over sectors. Because of the role of patents in protecting property rights some sectors have a higher propensity to patent than other sectors for strategic reasons (such as pharmaceuticals). Other sectors, such as the engineering sectors, produce a high number of innovations, but undertake relatively little formalized R&D because of the nature of production and innovation in that sector. Chapter 4 considers sector variations in a number of proxies for the UK, including an actual innovation count, in more detail, and finds important cross-sector differences. However, cross-country studies at the national level show a close correlation between levels of R&D expenditure and foreign patenting activity per capita (Soete, 1981; Fagerberg, 1987).[6] As a result, variations in the proxies may be more problematic for studies across sectors than across countries. Because of the close correlation between R&D and foreign patents they cannot be used together in the same model, but in order to take account of the different aspects of innovation which the two proxies cover, Fagerberg (1988) has used a weighted combination of them. This was based on civil R&D expenditure as a percentage of GDP, and external patents per capita adjusted for the openness of the economy. While a joint indicator may capture the benefits of both the variables used, the problem of how to combine them does remain. One alternative is to repeat the same model substituting the two proxies in order to control for sector and country variations which occur as a result of using a different proxy. In Verspagen and Wakelin (1997a) the sign and significance of the technology variable in explaining trade performance in the high-technology sector of computers varies with the choice of proxy used, appearing positively significant with patents and negative with R&D. Fagerberg (1994b) estimated the model with both R&D expenditure and a foreign patent variable as the technology variables, although in most cases only one was retained. Chapter 4 investigates this variation over proxies for the OECD countries.

Fagerberg (1987, 1988) corrected the patent variable used in the model for the openness and the size of the economy. The number of foreign patents was divided by population, and exports as a proportion of GDP. Verspagen (1993) tested the relationship between population, openness, R&D and patenting. He found an approximately linear relationship between openness and size and patents, indicating that a linear adjustment for openness is appropriate. In order to control for openness, Verspagen (1993) corrected the patent share of country j with its market share in the US relative to the market share of the other countries in the US as the denominator, this would be more than (less than) one for countries with above average (below average) trade with the US. As an alternative, patent shares were also corrected for relative population as well as relative market shares in the US market.

Verspagen (1993) also included labour productivity as an indication of technology along with the patent index, in order to capture the cost-reducing nature of process innovations. In another attempt to combine different aspects of innovation, Peretto (1990) devised a sectoral indicator of the 'opportunity to learn'. This was made by summing cumulative R&D expenditure for the latest three years with cumulative value added produced for the same period, and dividing by the number of operatives. The aim was to measure firms' learning opportunities both through formal R&D expenditure and via production.[7]

Aquino (1981) also used a combined technology index, combining cumulative discounted R&D expenditure, innovation counts and the wage rate at the country level. The results showed little variation between using this combined technology index and using the GDP of the country. Clearly, this is partly due to the level of aggregation considered (the country level) for which the technology index has already been aggregated over sectors, although it provides some justification for the widespread use of GDP in country-level studies as a proxy for 'development' or technological sophistication.

Another weakness of both R&D and patent variables is that they are flow variables, measuring flows into the stock of a country's technological capabilities rather than the stock of knowledge itself. Other studies have dealt with this problem by calculating stock variables either for patents (Cotsomitis et al., 1991) or for R&D expenditure (Buxton et al., 1991). The rationale is that skills and knowledge are embodied in past R&D as well as present, so that both should be taken account of when constructing a proxy. The problems in constructing a stock variable are in choosing the starting value and the most appropriate depreciation rate. In order to avoid these problems, Greenhalgh et al. (1994) created a 'quasi-stock measure' by constructing a moving average of the time series, with a variable lag.

Using a completely different approach, Antonelli (1986) suggests that the poor performance of technology theories of trade in non-science-based sectors is due to problems in the proxy. In order to avoid the use of a proxy altogether, he directly estimated the rate of diffusion of a shuttleless loom using S-shaped curves. Shuttleless looms represent an important process technology within the textile industry, normally considered a sector in which relative endowments of labour and capital play much more of a role in trade performance than differences in technology. The rate of diffusion was used as a determinant of trade performance in the textile industry across 28 countries in place of the usual proxies for technological change. The results 'confirmed that the capacity of a country to adopt new production process, capital equipment and intermediary products timely is a major determinant of its performance on international markets' (Antonelli, 1986, p. 79), thus the neo-technology theories of trade can also be applied to non-science-based sectors, in which the H–O–S theory is considered more appropriate. It is the use of a diffusion rate, rather than the standard input or output technology indicators which is crucial to the results.

An alternative source of technology indicator is to use the actual number of innovations, normally gathered from a survey. The problem with this method, which provides a direct count of innovations, is that it is generally only for one country and therefore provides an absolute measure of innovation, rather than a relative one. In addition, the problem of the variation in quality found with other proxies is not solved using an innovation count. For instance, for the Science Policy Research Unit (SPRU) survey of the UK, used in this book and by Greenhalgh (1990) and Greenhalgh et al. (1992, 1994), only significant innovations were chosen by a panel of experts. However, even within the sample of significant innovations there is likely to be a great deal of variation in their importance: one might be a radical breakthrough, while another has more limited economic application, but they are given the same weight when aggregate innovation counts are used.

To summarize, foreign patents and R&D expenditure are the most commonly used proxies for innovation. Because of the nature of innovation as a risky process, and the drawbacks of using R&D expenditure, output measures of innovation have generally been preferred in the literature considering the impact of technology on international trade. The alternative of using innovation counts is an interesting one, but retains the serious drawback of giving an absolute rather than relative measure of innovation. Attempts to survey innovations across countries are one solution to this problem.

3.4 SUMMARY

In recent years the dynamic impact of technology on trade performance has started to be tested. Static tests have already pointed to a role for technology gaps in explaining trade performance, particularly in some sectors; more recent attempts to test the dynamic implications of technology attest to the important long-run impact of technology on trade performance. These results have repercussions for the debate over the long-term convergence of countries in terms of growth. If differences in technology can have a long-term impact on growth, then international differences in the commitment of resources to innovation, and variations in international experience of innovation and hence learning, can lead to variations in growth performance. A country's specialization pattern, in sectors with either high or low levels of technological opportunity, can influence the country's growth pattern. The existence of technology gaps between countries which influence trade performance can thus have an impact on long-term trade and growth performance.

Finally, it is worth mentioning the problem of causality between trade and innovation. It may be that the sectors most exposed to international competition, that is, those with a high propensity to export, have a greater incentive to innovate, so that causation can run from exports to innovation.

Hughes (1986) considers a simultaneous equation model of R&D expenditure and exports for the UK. She found some evidence for the simultaneity of the relationship between exports and R&D expenditure in a cross-section of industries. However, Greenhalgh et al. (1994), using patents and counts of innovation as the innovation variables for a UK model over both sectors and time, found that 'simultaneity between the innovation measures used here and net export performance does not appear likely to be significant' (p. 112). Most of the static models have considered the causation between lagged innovation and trade performance, ruling out the possibility of simultaneity through the use of lagged innovation variables.

NOTES

1. This is the Balassa (1965) index which gives a country's performance in sector i relative to the same country's performance in total trade, and therefore shows the trade specialization pattern.
2. Kaldor found a positive (and therefore 'perverse') relationship between growth in unit labour costs and growth in export market shares for a number of countries from 1963 to 1975. Amendola et al. (1993) find that the effects of labour costs on trade performance only occur in the short run. They conclude that the relationship found by Kaldor was a 'spurious correlation' which disappears once the dynamics are correctly specified and technology is included in the model.
3. This leads to another inconsistency. For the trade flows between 14 countries there should be 91 bilateral relationships ($(n*(n-1))/2$), the authors use double this number, implying that they have used the same trade flow in two directions, which given the symmetry of the model is the same as using each pair of observations twice. This would imply that the number of significant coefficients was always even, whereas the authors obtained uneven results for some coefficients.
4. There are also some models which consider the data pooled.
5. The benefits and drawbacks of patent-based proxies are discussed in detail in Chapter 4.
6. Greenhalgh et al. (1994) found little temporal correlation between R&D and either innovations or patents for the UK from 1970 to 1983.
7. Amendola et al. (1993) consider patents as acting as a proxy for disembodied technical change, while fixed investment captures learning and innovations in capital equipment, that is, embodied technical change.

PART II

Technology and Inter-country Trade

4. Trade and Innovation in the European Union

The aim of this chapter is to test for the influence of technology gaps on bilateral intra-European trade performance. Six bilateral relationships between four European countries – France, West Germany, the Netherlands and the UK – are considered, with an extension to the bilateral trade of all the EU countries with West Germany. The first four countries are all advanced industrialized countries at a similar stage of development, and important mutual trading partners, linked institutionally through the process of European union. It is precisely in these circumstances – of high levels of trade between countries with similar capital to labour endowments – that alternatives to the factor proportions theory of trade have been sought; and to which the original theory of technology gaps (Posner, 1961) was addressed. This chapter abstracts from other possible sources of trade and presents some preliminary evidence as to the importance of differences in innovation in affecting intra-European trade performance at a detailed sector level.

Emphasis is placed on the economic 'convergence' of the European countries as a pre-condition to the process of integration within Europe. The convergence criteria that countries must fulfil in order to proceed to full monetary union, as set out in the Maastricht Treaty, concentrate on financial macroeconomic goals such as the level of the budget deficit and the rate of inflation. However, differences in innovation levels and in the commitment of resources to innovation remain a fundamental source of divergence between European countries, as well as a potential explanation for variations in trade performance.[1] The relationship considered in this chapter is a static one, examining technology gaps as a basis for trade in a single year; however, technology gaps also have important dynamic implications for differences in growth between European countries. The existence of technology gaps within Europe, and possibly between some of the most-developed European countries, has implications for science and technology policy at both the national and the European level. Linking innovation to poor trade performance gives technology policy a vital role within a wider industrial policy; differences in innovation performance at the European level indicate a serious impediment to 'real' economic convergence.

The chapter is divided into three main parts. The first of these sets out the technology gap hypothesis, outlines the benefits and drawbacks of using foreign patents as a proxy for innovation, and outlines some descriptive statistics for the four European countries under consideration. Some evidence of the relationship between patents, R&D expenditure and actual innovations for the UK is presented. The second section presents some correlations between trade performance and relative innovation on a bilateral basis, both for each bilateral flow and according to the source country. The results indicate a positive and significant relationship between relative innovation and trade performance for France and Germany but not for the Netherlands and the UK. Re-estimating the model using export shares in the EU as the dependent variable confirms the earlier results. Finally, the bilateral trade flows of all the EU countries with West Germany are considered; a separation between the less- and more-developed countries seems evident. The latter group shows a closer relationship between trade performance and differences in innovation. In the subsection which follows, the model is re-estimated on a sectoral basis, pooling the bilateral trade flows across countries and years, and estimating the relationship separately for each of the forty sectors. The results find a strong positive correlation between relative innovation and trade performance for half the sectors considered, indicating an important role in trade performance; the relationship varies considerably over both countries and sectors. The last section presents some conclusions.

4.1 THE TECHNOLOGY GAP HYPOTHESIS

The hypothesis to be considered in this chapter is that differences in innovation (technology gaps) are an important determinant of differences in trade performance between countries. The analysis looks at a static relationship between bilateral differences in innovation and bilateral trade performance. Technology gaps may characterize the aggregate trading relationship between countries (one country is technologically superior to another in all sectors), or they may only exist in particular sectors for each country. In order to take account of the potentially sector-specific nature of technology gaps, it is necessary to test the relationship using sector-level data.

Some observers believe that as aggregate income levels converge, and countries become more similar, differences in innovation become a less important source of trade. This view is expressed by Deardorff (1984, p. 499):

There is also some question as to whether the role of technology, whatever it has been in the past, may be diminishing in importance for explaining patterns of trade that are emerging today . . . it will be interesting to see whether the existing technology theories of trade will be refined and convincingly tested before they are left behind by a changing world.

This point of view assumes that, in the changing world, differences in innovation are of decreasing importance. This is presumably based on the belief that differences in innovation are less likely to occur between developed countries at similar income levels; that convergence in real incomes, combined with economic integration through trade, decreases the possibility of technology gaps existing between countries.

This chapter wishes to question that point of view by considering technology gaps between four developed European countries which are also highly integrated through trade and foreign direct investment. According to one point of view, this high level of integration indicates that there are many available channels for the diffusion of innovation between these countries, which in turn implies that technology gaps can exist only in the short run. An alternative viewpoint, in keeping with an evolutionary view of innovation, with its emphasis on the cumulative and tacit nature of technological change, sees the advantages of innovation accumulating over time. In part this is due to the path-dependent nature of technological change, with past occurrences affecting innovation in the present. As a result, a country with a past history of innovation in a particular field may continue to have a competitive advantage in that field through learning and experience. This view implies that technology gaps can also occur between developed integrated economies, and that differences in innovation can continue to exert an influence on trade over time. Although *scientific* knowledge may be freely available through scientific journals and the links of the academic community, the ability to exploit technological opportunities in each field varies considerably between different countries (Archibugi and Pianta, 1992).

The analysis is a static one, considering trade performance for 1987. Ideally, data are required at the sector level for a number of countries in order to test the technology gap hypothesis, allowing differences in innovation across countries to be considered. In this chapter the data are both country and sector specific and are considered on a bilateral basis; the bilateral flows are taken individually and by the country of origin, as well as grouped by sector. This chapter covers the same 40 sectors as in Soete (1981, 1987), but considers the relationship on a bilateral rather than a cross-country basis.

One of the first tests of the technology gap model across countries (Hufbauer, 1970) used time (shown by the first trade date) to test if the production of new products relates to exports. A proxy for relative innovation (based on patents) is preferred here, as an indication of relative sectoral technological capability. Two different specifications of the patent variable are used. The problem of finding an internationally comparable proxy for innovation is reviewed in the following subsection. The subsequent subsections give some descriptive statistics for the sample countries' aggregate patterns of trade and innovation.

4.1.1 Patents as an Innovation Proxy

The two main proxies for innovation used in economic studies are patents and R&D expenditure, although others (such as the number of scientific personnel and actual counts of innovation) are also available. Despite being widely used as a proxy for innovation, R&D expenditure is an input into the innovative process rather than an output from it. The exact relationship between expenditure on research and the output of innovations from that research is generally uncertain, and is likely to vary greatly according to the characteristics of both the unit undertaking the research (for example, a government research agency or a firm) and the characteristics of the technology itself. The use of R&D expenditure as a proxy for innovation involves making some assumptions about this relationship.

Patents, on the other hand, are an output from the innovation process and have been widely used in industrial economics.[2] Griliches (1990) points out that patents, as an output from the innovative process, involve some estimation of the stochastic variation which can be assumed to make up part of technical change and which is not captured by R&D expenditure. This conceptualization of R&D as an input, and patents as the intermediate output, suggests that a strong correlation should be found between them. Scherer (1983), using a sample of 4,274 individual company lines of business, showed the probability of patenting increases with R&D expenditure, and there is a high correlation between a firm having no R&D expenditure and producing no patents. At the industry level he found a close proportional relationship between the two for the majority of sectors, but a non-linear relationship, generally with diminishing returns to R&D, for a minority of them. Acs and Audretsch (1989) estimated the relationship between patents (the dependent variable) and R&D expenditure and other variables, including the concentration ratio and indications of the level of knowledge such as R&D personnel. The relationship was estimated for the US, at a detailed level of 147 sectors, and repeated earlier work (Acs and Audretsch, 1988) which used the same model but with the actual number of innovations; this allows the behaviour of patents and actual innovations to be contrasted. R&D was positively and significantly related to patents; company R&D was more significant than total R&D, which included both government and company R&D. The same relationship was found with the number of innovations. The results indicate that for the US there appears to be a strong correlation between patents, R&D expenditure and actual innovations.

The use of patent data involves either an explicit or an implicit assumption as to what type of activity they actually measure: invention (the inception of an idea prior to its commercial development); or innovation (the subsequent application of the idea commercially). The second stage, that of innovation, is of greater economic significance, as it involves the utilization of a new technique that may alter the production possibilities within a firm or industry. Whether patents reflect invention or innovation depends at what stage of the process they are taken out. A study by Basberg (1982) of the whaling industry shows that patenting activity reached its peak at the time of first commercial exploitation rather than earlier, implying that patents are responding to economic conditions and reflect innovation. It will be assumed for the purposes of this study that patents are a proxy for innovative, not just inventive, activity.

Using patents in an international study introduces another form of non-compatibility: each country has its own legal and bureaucratic arrangements for the granting of patents, influencing the propensity to patent in that country. One way of compensating for this problem is to use patents granted to each country in a third country, so that all applications will go through the same screening process. The cost and time needed to take out a patent abroad may also ensure that the patents are all of a certain quality.[3] This is especially true if the third country is an important technology centre such as the United States where 48 per cent of the patents granted in 1988 were to foreign inventors, the highest number of overseas patents in the OECD. Soete and Wyatt (1983) found a strong positive relationship between domestic R&D expenditure and foreign patenting; they suggest that foreign patenting has considerable advantages as an indicator of innovation. Soete (1987) examined the relationship between foreign patenting (in five industrialized countries), domestic patenting and domestic R&D expenditure. He found that both foreign patenting and domestic patenting were highly correlated with domestic R&D, and in the case of three of the foreign patent markets (including the US) foreign patenting obtained better results than domestic patenting. He concluded that foreign patenting, particularly in the US, provides a good proxy for innovation.

However, there are some difficulties associated with the use of foreign patents. For instance, the propensity to patent in the US may be influenced by the level of trade with the US, as the expected market share influences firms' willingness to take out patents. As a result, foreign patents would reflect the importance of the export market, instead of reflecting national innovation levels. In order to correct for the influence of trade on the number of foreign patents taken out by countries, Fagerberg (1987, 1988) corrected the number of foreign patents by the level of trade with the world. One problem with correcting for openness is that the exact relationship between openness and patenting is not clear. Verspagen (1993) estimated a patenting function for 37 countries including both OECD countries and 13 NICs. Using a Cobb–Douglas function to estimate the relationship between R&D expenditure, country size (shown by population) and the openness of the economy, Verspagen found the elasticities for size and openness to be approximately one, so that it appears reasonable to assume a linear relationship between the two variables and patenting. It is presumed that correcting for openness is not necessary for this sample of countries, given the similarity of the trade patterns of the countries considered.[4] Basberg (1983) found no significant relationship between Norway's patenting in the US and its exports to the US. Instead, patenting in the US appeared to reflect domestic innovation patterns rather than being influenced by the importance of the foreign export market.

The propensity to patent abroad has also increased during the post-war years. Kitti and Schiffel (1978) have shown that for most industrialized countries the share of foreign patents has risen; they conclude that this trend reflects both increasing international economic interdependence and rivalry. Pavitt (1982) found that despite this growth, national rankings of the growth of foreign patenting and the growth of R&D expenditure remained 'virtually the same' among the OECD countries. This indicates that the rise in the propensity to patent in the US has not varied systematically across the OECD countries. Another variation in patenting over time is that the level of patents granted may vary with changes in the bureaucratic or legal system; one example (Griliches, 1990) is the influence of changes in funding of the US patent office on the number of patents issued in the US. This difficulty is most significant for attempts to use patents as time series over long time periods, although such variations should affect all countries equally. The propensity to patent abroad also relies on domestic patenting and business practices. One extreme example of this is the low propensity to patent of the ex-USSR and the centrally planned economies of Eastern Europe. Such differences are less likely to exist between industrialized countries.

There remain, however, a number of significant failings in the use of patents as a proxy for innovation. First, not all innovations are patentable; second, not all innovations that are patentable are patented; and third, those that are vary greatly in quality. The first two problems may also vary by the sector leading to inter-industry differences in patenting, according to the economic incentives to patent in that industry. Factors which are important in influencing the propensity to patent are the degree of monopoly power, average firm size and the characteristics of the product and production process. Mansfield (1981) showed that patents are often taken out to protect innovations against potential imitators; thus patenting activity varies with the level of protection afforded by the patent relative to other methods and to the level of competition in the sector. Scherer (1983) explains the low propensity to patent in the aircraft and automobile industries as due to the importance of prototypes in the former and styling improvements in the latter, neither of which give rise to many patents. Overall he found high concentration and relatively high levels of government-backed R&D expenditure to be related to a low propensity to patent. This shows the often strategic nature of patent applications; they may involve the 'blocking' of further innovation through the exertion of the monopoly power conferred by the patent. Significant factors that may influence the decision to apply for a patent include a rapidly changing market, or the short life expectancy of a product, both of which alter the strategic pay-offs from patenting.

In addition, using the number of patents produced in a sector as an indication of technological change within the sector ignores the impact of innovations originating outside the sector. As Robson et al. (1988) have shown for the UK, a few core sectors (such as instruments and electronics) are of prime importance in the production of technology which is then used in a much broader selection of industries, including non-manufacturing. They note that sectoral interdependence in innovation shows a rising trend in the UK, particularly because of the importance of electronic-based new technologies widely applied outside their industry of origin. The industrial structure of the economy influences the pattern of technological diffusion from one sector to another, creating a national system of innovation. As a result, technological development in one sector will encourage the growth of related sectors. Inter-sectoral flows of innovation are not captured by sector-specific patent counts; indeed, patents act to prevent the process of diffusion through protection which provides a barrier to diffusion[5] (Verspagen, 1993).

The variation in the quality of the innovations indicated by the patents is a problem common to most proxies of innovation, including direct counts of innovation. While some innovations may present radical departures from past production methods, or important new products, others represent incremental improvements to existing products and processes, or inventions with no economic impact. By giving each patent equal weight this heterogeneity in quality is not taken account of.[6] For international studies, if the quality of innovations varies systematically over countries then this constitutes a serious drawback. Assuming that these cross-country variations in quality do not occur, the law of large numbers can be invoked to consider the variations in quality; as a result the economic value of any patent will be a random variable with a probability distribution (Scherer, 1984).

The relationship between innovation, R&D and foreign patenting is considered here using data for the UK on both the actual number of innovations (taken from the SPRU survey of innovations, details of which are given in Chapters 5 and 6) and cumulative R&D expenditure and US patents. Correlations are made to consider the relationship between patents and R&D expenditure, and between patents and counts of actual innovations. The latter are provided in two classifications, one is by the sector of the firm which produced the innovation (*PROD*) and the other by the sector of the first user of the innovation (*USER*); these data are from 1945–83. The sectoral distribution of innovations over time is very stable; using the last five years of the period makes no significant difference to the results. Cumulative R&D (from 1973 to 1990), and cumulative patents (from 1973 to 1987) are also examined; these long periods are taken to smooth the data for any indivisibilities (this refers particularly to the patent data) which may cause seemingly large variations between years. The correlations between them made across 18 manufacturing sectors for the UK are given below in Table 4.1, the standard errors are given in parentheses.

While the correlation between the production of innovations (*PROD*) and patents shows a strong relationship with a high explanatory power, the correlation between patents and the use of innovation is positive and significant (at 8 per cent), but the explanatory power is much lower. This indicates that patents are a good proxy for the pattern of innovation, but are not as effective in capturing the diffusion of innovation to sectors other than the sector in which the innovation was produced.

The relationship between patents and R&D expenditure is also weaker than that between patents and innovations produced. Part of the reason for this is that the machinery sector is an outlier, having by far the highest output of patents but being relatively non-R&D intensive. As others have pointed out (Robson et al., 1988), this is due to innovations occurring as a result of production in the machinery sector, rather than through formal R&D, so that the latter underestimates innovation in this sector. Repeating the correlation excluding the machinery sector results in a positive relationship between patents and R&D, although this remains weaker than the relationship between innovation and patents.

Table 4.1 Correlations between innovation proxies

Equation estimated	R^2
Patents = 96 (867) + 25.7 (2.88)*** *PROD*	0.83
Patents = 2,183 (2,212) + 22.5 (12.38)* *USER*	0.17
Patents = 3,994 (2,032) + 0.34 (0.37) *R&D*	0.05
Patents = 2,540 (1,029) + 0.38 (0.18)** *R&D* (excluding machinery)	0.22

Notes
*** Significant at 1%, ** at 5%, * at 10%.

To summarize, there are a number of drawbacks in taking patents as an indicator of innovation. Using foreign in place of domestic patents reduces some of these problems, but also introduces new ones, such as the question of causation between trade and foreign patents. Overall, however, in the imperfect world of choosing an innovation proxy, foreign patents are a valuable source of information and appear to be a good proxy for direct innovation. There is some evidence that they may be less appropriate for the diffusion of innovation. It is the output of new innovations that the technology gap theory emphasizes (Soete, 1981), and as a result it is appropriate to use an output measure, such as a patent-based indicator of innovation, when considering the technology gap hypothesis.

4.1.2 Innovation in the European Union

The European countries' innovation patterns are diverse. European R&D expenditure is dominated by West Germany, accounting for 36 per cent in 1983, while the Netherlands expenditure constitutes less than 5 per cent (figures from the OECD). When this is evaluated on a per capita basis, Germany still spends more than other European countries; France and the Netherlands are at a similar but lower level, and the UK lags slightly behind all three. With R&D as a percentage of value added the German advantage is still clear, but the UK has reversed positions with France and the Netherlands. However, it is the growth of R&D expenditure that provides the clearest example of diversity. While Germany and France have maintained per annum growth of more than 5 per cent from 1967 to 1983, the UK and the Netherlands have had per annum rates of 1 per cent and 2 per cent respectively. Given that convergence would require faster growth rates from those countries with a lower innovation base, this combination of high (low) levels of R&D and high (low) growth rates of R&D is not conducive to the idea of economic convergence. This diversity within Europe has been emphasized by Patel and Pavitt (1987), who highlight the underlying differences between countries arising from their differing attitudes to R&D expenditure.

The aggregate nature of these statistics on R&D expenditure does not reveal the sectoral distribution of the expenditure. The level of expenditure on defence is important in this respect, and varies greatly across the countries in this sample. The UK and France spend 21 per cent and 29 per cent respectively of their R&D expenditure on defence (in 1987), while this figure is much lower for the other two countries of the sample. When it comes to assessing innovation, military research is unlikely to generate as many patents as other types of research because of its confidential nature, and may in general be less market-orientated, limiting the diffusion of new inventions from this sector to the rest of the economy.

This point is also shown in the shares of each of the different countries in patenting within the sample. West Germany dominates patenting, providing almost half (47.4 per cent) of the patents taken out in the US by the sample countries in 1984; this reflects its larger contribution to research within Europe. The statistics for patenting per million of population also show West Germany ahead (78 per million), with the Netherlands a close second (73), then France (52); the UK (30 patents per million) significantly lags behind the other countries. The high figure for the Netherlands may reflect the importance of multinational companies which have a high propensity to patent abroad, because of their international scope.

4.1.3 Trade Patterns in the European Union

All four of the countries in the sample are open economies in which trade is a significant part of the economy. The importance of intra-EU trade for each of the four countries is clearly shown for 1987 in Table 4.2. In the case of each country, intra-EU trade constitutes more than half of total exports and imports (UK exports are almost exactly half). The UK and West Germany appear to be less orientated to intra-EU trade than France and the Netherlands, while the latter country – presumably because of its small size – has a large dependency on EU export markets with 75 per cent of its exports going to other EU countries.

In order to examine the stability of each country's pattern of bilateral trade with the other countries in the sample, the bilateral trade performance for each pair of countries was calculated across forty industries for two separate years, 1987 and 1979. Correlations between the trade performances of 1987 and 1979 were then made. The correlations are generally high, with coefficients above 0.8 for all the bilateral flows (with the exception of the Netherlands with the UK) showing relatively little change in the pattern of bilateral flows over the eight-year period.

Table 4.2 Intra-EU trade flows as a percentage of trade

	Total exports to EU (%)	Total imports from EU (%)
Netherlands	75.4	61.5
France	60.4	65.6
W. Germany	52.7	54.6
UK	49.2	51.2

Closer observation of the relationship between the Netherlands and the UK shows that the balance of trade has been reversed for a number of industries. The trade balance improved for the Netherlands over all industries with two exceptions: petroleum went from a positive balance (0.54) in 1979 to a negative balance (–0.57) in 1987, and there was a small decrease in shipbuilding. The increase in the UK's exports of petroleum is one of the most noticeable changes in the export pattern of the countries considered. From 1973 onwards, the UK became a major exporter of petroleum and natural gas. Dalum (1992), in his study of the stability of national systems of innovation over time, noted that the UK has experienced a large change in export specialization over the period 1961–87 because of the rise in oil exports. The other three countries in the sample, however, have been characterized by stable export specialization patterns over the same period.

One way to give a preliminary indication of the relationship between trade and innovation is to examine the pattern of trade according to technological content. The trade flows can be classified by technological content by weighing them according to R&D intensity. The index used here is based on the OECD division of industries by their technology level (defined using R&D intensity) denoted by the values of 3 for high technology (R&D intense), 2 for medium and 1 for low. The importance of each type of industry for the exports of each country to the other was then calculated, providing a weighting for the technology index. That is, aggregated to give an indication of the R&D intensity of total trade, a higher intensity implying a higher level of the index. The results for 1987 using this categorization are given in Table 4.3.

Table 4.3 Trade by R&D intensity for 1987

Exporter	Importer country				
	France	NL	Germany	UK	Average
France	–	1.69	1.70	1.71	1.70
NL	1.58	–	1.41	1.66	1.55
Germany	1.88	1.66	–	1.84	1.79
UK	1.64	1.54	1.69	–	1.62

This method has weaknesses because of the variations in the level of technology used within each sector, and between the same sector in different countries (Soete, 1987). Basing the technology level of a sector on the OECD (1986) average R&D intensity in that sector fails to reflect any factor intensity differences that exist between countries, assuming that the sector is characterized by the same R&D intensity in each country.

The low R&D intensity of Dutch/German trade is clearly demonstrated. Dutch exports to Germany had the lowest R&D intensity in 1987 and also in 1979. The highest was for German exports to France in 1987 (followed by German exports to the UK), whereas in 1979 it was German exports to the UK (followed by UK exports to France). Overall, considering the distribution of trade between technology levels (not shown here) the only clear specialization demonstrated on the basis of R&D intensity is that Germany specializes in medium-technology industries, and has the highest average level of R&D intensity in its exports. The Netherlands appears to export the least R&D-intensive products, while the UK has experienced a fall in the R&D intensity of its exports with respect to the 1979 results. These patterns fit in with the R&D expenditure situation considered earlier, with Germany investing considerably more than the other countries in research, France exhibiting growth in its R&D expenditure, and the UK stagnation.

To summarize, the sample countries are heterogeneous, both in terms of their aggregate innovation levels (shown by patenting and R&D expenditure) and the R&D intensity of their bilateral exports. They are important mutual trading partners, and the patterns of trade between them appear to be relatively stable over time. The next section investigates the relationship between their relative innovation patterns and bilateral trade performance.

4.2 A MODEL OF TRADE AND INNOVATION

Three different analyses are made in this section. The first considers the bilateral relationships between the countries on the basis of each bilateral flow and by the source country; the second uses a multilateral export variable – the share of exports in the EU – to check the results; and the third extends the analysis to all European bilateral flows with West Germany.

4.2.1 A Bilateral Country Analysis

In order to test the impact of differences in innovation on trade performance, correlations are made between bilateral trade performance and relative innovation. A positive relationship is expected between trade performance (for 1987) and the patent variables. Two different patent variables are used, lagged by four years as a delay is expected between the taking out of a patent and its impact on production and trade.[7] The appropriate length of the lag is unclear, as patenting may occur at different stages of the innovative process. Van Hulst et al. (1991) set the time lag at two to six years, but argue that the length of the lag is unimportant, as the level of innovation changes only slowly over time, making the results insensitive to the length of the lag chosen. For this sample of countries correlations of the patent index for each country over time for 1984 and 1980, showed little change (for both Germany and the Netherlands the correlations are 1, for France 0.98, and for the UK 0.93), indicating little variation in the pattern of innovation during the 1980s. As a result we would not expect the results to be sensitive to the lag chosen.

The relationship is estimated for each bilateral relationship over 40 sectors for 1987 and is given below in equation (4.1):

$$TP_{pqs} = \alpha + \beta\,INN_{pqs} + \varepsilon \qquad (4.1)$$

where TP is net bilateral trade performance between countries p and q given by the difference in the exports of the two countries in sector s over the sum of their exports in sector i:

$$TP_{pqs} = \frac{X_{pqs} - X_{qps}}{X_{pqs} + X_{qps}}$$

where X is exports.[8] This index is bounded by plus or minus one and implicitly takes into account the transportability of the product, which will affect both countries equally. However, the index gives no indication of the importance of each industry in overall trade, as it reflects only trade performance in that industry relative to another country. The use of net rather than gross trade abstracts from the proportion of intra-industry trade in total trade. *INN* is an indicator of relative innovation between the two countries, and is based on patents taken out in the US by each country. Two different patent indices are used. The first is the ratio of per capita average patents (from 1981–84) between the two countries p and q. This is given by:

$$PAT_{pqs} = \frac{PAT_{ps}/POP_p}{PAT_{qs}/POP_q}$$

averages are taken in order to smooth for yearly variations, which may appear large because of the small number of patents taken out in some industries in some years. Weighting the number of patents by population (*POP*) takes account of the relative size of the two countries. The second innovation proxy used is the difference in the revealed technological advantage indices (*RTA*) for the two countries. The *RTA* index gives country p's share of patents granted in the US in sector s relative to the rest of the EU countries, over the country's total patent share in the US for all sectors and is given below.[9]

$$RTA_{ps} = \frac{PAT_{ps}/\sum_{\pi} PAT_{ps}}{\sum_{\sigma} PAT_{ps}/\sum_{\sigma}\sum_{\pi} PAT_{ps}}$$

A value higher than one shows a comparative advantage for country p in industry s, and a value less than one a comparative disadvantage. There are a number of relevant features to this index. First, it is comparative not absolute, every country has an advantage in something. Second, countries specializing in high-technology goods will not have higher average indices than less-advanced nations, as the index does not reflect the absolute number of patents. It is a well-defined specialization pattern which gives a high index, so those countries with a definite pattern of revealed technological advantage (such as small countries) may have higher indices for some sectors. For these reasons, the first index of relative patents per capita is more appropriate for a test of the technology gap model, and will be preferred *a priori* to the ratio of *RTA* indices. Two proxies are used in order to control for variations due to the specific formulation of the patent index. The results from the correlations are given in the first six rows of Table 4.4 for both innovation proxies; the first three columns give the results for the difference in *RTA* indices, and the last three columns using the ratio of per capita patents, standard errors are given in parentheses. There is a positive and significant relationship for three out of six of the bilateral relationships (at less than 5 per cent) using the proxy PAT. In addition the relationship between the Netherlands and the UK is significant (at 10 per cent), but with the opposite sign from that expected, indicating that the trade performance between the two countries is negatively related to their relative innovation pattern, that is, areas of relative innovation are associated with poor trade performance.

The results vary a little between the two proxies, reflecting their different formulations. The absolute differences in innovation, shown by the *PAT* index, play a significant role in explaining trade performance between France and the Netherlands, France and Germany, and the Netherlands and Germany. It is noticeable that none of the relationships involving the UK appears to have a significant relationship between trade performance and relative innovation.

These results are not consistent with the results of Hughes (1986). Considering UK–German bilateral trade for 1978, she found a positive and significant role for differences in R&D expenditure. There are a number of differences between the model tested here and Hughes (1986). First, they are separated by nine years and the relationship may have changed over time; second, one uses a patent index rather than R&D expenditure as the innovation proxy; third the Hughes' model includes a number of other explanatory variables, the lack of which in this chapter may bias the results. Finally the Hughes study considers 16 sectors while the results presented here are for 40 sectors.

The bilateral flows can also be grouped according to the source country of the flow (including three bilateral flows for each country of origin), to give source-country, rather than bilateral, summaries of the results. These correlations are shown in the last four rows of Table 4.4, again using both innovation proxies.

The results fall into two groups, and are consistent across the two proxies. The results with France and Germany as the source countries appear to have positive and significant relationships between relative innovation and bilateral trade performance; for the UK and the Netherlands relative innovation does not appear to be an important factor in influencing trade performance. Referring to Table 4.3, showing the relative R&D intensities of their bilateral flows, a correspondence can be seen between countries which have their trade more influenced by innovation and the average R&D intensity of their trade. France and Germany had more R&D-intensive trade flows, and also appear to have a closer relationship between relative innovation and trade performance. Clearly this does not account for their trade flows with other countries, but only bilaterally within this sample.

In contrast, van Hulst et al. (1991), for the same period, find a positive and significant correlation between two export variables – export specialization and the export/import ratio – and technological specialization (shown by the *RTA* index) for the Netherlands. The results for the other countries showed that Germany had a positive correlation when some sector-specific dummies were included; no correlation was found for France and the UK was not included in the sample. They considered only 19 sectors rather than the 40 considered here, which may have influenced the results. Soete (1987) found a positive and significant relationship between patent intensity and export performance only for Germany out of the countries in the sample; in fact the Netherlands had a negative relationship between net exports and patenting.

This preliminary evidence from the bilateral relationships seems to support the existence of technology gaps on a bilateral basis between European countries, although they do not characterize all intra-European trade flows. The four countries considered here seem to fall into two categories, the first of which (France and Germany) has a positive relationship between relative innovation and trade performance, while for the second (the Netherlands and the UK) no such relationship appears to exist. This internal diversity among EU countries is emphasized in Archibugi and Pianta's 1992 study of the 'national systems of innovation' of the European countries. They observe that there are considerable differences among European countries in terms of history, and economic performance, and that treating Europe as a single unit risks ignoring this diversity. It would seem that the particular national system

Table 4.4 Results for bilateral and country trade flows

Proxy	RTA			PAT		
	α	INN	R^2 / F	α	INN	R^2 / F
France–NL	-0.02 (0.06)	0.50 (0.48)	0.03 1.08	-0.15 (0.08)	0.10** (0.04)	0.11 4.58**
France–Germany	-0.21 (0.04)	0.79*** (0.26)	0.19 9.34***	-0.37 (0.07)	0.20*** (0.07)	0.17 7.89***
France–UK	0.08 (0.05)	0.47* (0.29)	0.07 2.76*	0.01 (0.07)	0.03 (0.02)	0.05 1.93
NL–Germany	-0.24 (0.06)	0.48** (0.24)	0.10 4.19***	-0.36 (0.08)	0.12** (0.05)	0.13 5.44**
NL–UK	0.07 (0.05)	-0.47** (0.22)	0.10 4.43***	0.15 (0.07)	-0.08* (0.05)	0.07 2.78*
Germany–UK	0.32 (0.05)	0.001 (0.57)	0.00 0.00	0.32 (0.15)	0.001 (0.05)	0.00 0.01
France	-0.05 (0.03)	0.13*** (0.05)	0.07 8.31***	-0.15 (0.44)	0.08*** (0.02)	0.09 11.8***
NL	-0.05 (0.04)	0.03 (0.04)	0.00 0.28	-0.05 (0.05)	0.004 (0.02)	0.00 0.03
Germany	0.25 (0.03)	0.12*** (0.04)	0.08 10.4***	0.14 (0.04)	0.05*** (0.02)	0.06 7.02***
UK	-0.15 (0.03)	-0.04 (0.04)	0.01 0.80	-0.16 (0.04)	0.01 (0.04)	0.00 0.07

Notes:
*** t-statistic significant at 1%, ** significant at 5%, * significant at 10%.

of innovation of a country, which constitutes its structure of innovation strengths and weaknesses, still plays an important role in explaining relative trade performance.

4.2.2 Export Shares

In order to further investigate the results an alternative dependent variable was used based on each individual country's performance relative to the other countries. The dependent variable used is the share of exports of each country in each industry relative to intra-EU trade by the twelve EU countries in that sector. This gives a multilateral, rather than bilateral, indication of competitiveness within Europe, which given the importance of the European market to these countries can be used as a proxy for each country's competitiveness in general. Absolute differences in innovation between countries (influenced by their national systems of innovation) lead to changes in market shares on the European market. The export share is given by:

$$XSH_{ps} = \frac{X_{ps}}{\sum_{eu} X_s}$$

that is, country p's exports to the other EU countries in sector s, over total EU exports in that sector. Analogously a patent share index was used as the innovation proxy. As the export share is likely to vary with country size (with larger countries having a larger share of EU exports) the patent index was corrected for country size by taking the per capita patents of country p over the per capita patents of the four countries considered earlier. As they are the main source of patents in the EU this should be similar to total EU patenting in the US. Cumulative patents from 1973 to 1984 were used, in order to smooth for variations over time. Again, correlations were made between this patent index and export share for 1987; the results are given in Table 4.5.

The formulation of this model differs from that presented in Table 4.4; it reflects the relationship between the trade performance of each country relative to all the European Union countries.[10] Despite this alternative formulation, the results are consistent with the earlier ones presented in Table 4.4. France and Germany appear to have their intra-EU trade positively affected by relative innovation, and for the UK there appears to be no relationship between the two. For the Netherlands the results have changed, with some relationship existing between trade performance and innovation, perhaps on account of its trade performance with EU countries other than the three trading partners already considered. Using this alternative model the UK stands out as having no relationship at all between relative innovation and its competitiveness within Europe, indicating that factors other than technology are important in influencing the UK's export share within Europe.

Table 4.5 Export and patent shares

	α	INN	R^2 F
France	0.11	0.05 **	0.11
	(0.02)	(0.03)	4.56 **
NL	0.08	0.02 *	0.06
	(0.02)	(0.01)	2.42 *
Germany	0.23	0.07 *	0.07
	(0.05)	(0.04)	3.07 *
UK	0.14	0.02	0.00
	(0.05)	(0.08)	0.03

Notes:
** t-statistic significant at 5%, * significant at 10%.

Considerable empirical work has been done on the export performance of the UK, and in particular the role of innovation (see, for instance, Katrak, 1982; Greenhalgh, 1990; Temple, 1994). The rise in oil exports has certainly altered the UK's bilateral trade relationships, especially with oil importers such as the other three countries considered here. Walker (1993) has analysed the UK's national system of innovation and found it to be highly reliant on military expenditure (which has a positive effect on the aircraft and arms industries), and chemicals. As a consequence, out of the high-technology sectors only pharmaceuticals and aerospace can be considered 'strong performers' for the UK (Temple, 1994). The importance of military technology in the UK's national system of innovation may not be captured by the patent proxy, as many military innovations are not patented because of the desire for secrecy; this may partly explain the lack of correlation for the UK. As a result, the model was re-estimated leaving out two sectors – petroleum (26) and arms (6) – the former as it is not expected to be influenced by innovation, and the latter as patents do not accurately reflect innovation in this sector. Both these two industries are characterized by a high UK export share (57 per cent of European bilateral flows for arms, and 37 per cent for petroleum) but low levels of UK patenting. Re-estimating the model for export shares without these two observations leads to a positive and significant correlation (at 5 per cent) between export shares and the share of patenting, with an R^2 of 10 per cent. Thus it appears that although UK trade performance does not appear to be influenced by innovation shares, this is partly due to the influence of two observations, arms and petroleum; for other sectors there does appear to be a relationship between innovation and export performance.

4.2.3 European trade with West Germany

In order to extend the analysis to all European countries, this subsection returns to using bilateral trade, but this time for all the twelve EU countries' trade with respect to West Germany, as the presumed technological leader within Europe. While all the countries in the EU can be classified as developed, much of the discussion about the creation of a customs union has been concerned with the impact of union between countries at different stages of development. The less-developed countries, such as Portugal, Spain and Greece, have expressed concern at the technological rivalry of exports from the north of Europe, while other countries, such as the UK, France and Germany, have been concerned over competition from cheap imports coming from the lower-wage countries of the South. The bilateral trade patterns of each of the EU countries were calculated relative to Germany (there are nine, as Belgium and Luxembourg are taken together and Greece was not considered because of a lack of data), with Germany as the exporting country p and each other country as the partner country q. Both of the patent proxies are used, relative per capita patents and the difference in *RTA* indices. In some sectors some countries have taken out no patents in the US, and as a result the relative patent ratio cannot be calculated (as the denominator, the number of patents taken out by country q is zero). In order to get round this problem, in cases where the partner country has no patents, the per capita patents of Germany are taken alone (that is, the denominator, or the number of patents taken out by the partner country, is assumed to be one instead of zero). The bilateral flows with the three countries already considered (France, the Netherlands and the UK) are also included for clarity.

The results (presented in the first nine rows of Table 4.6) show considerable variation both across countries, and across the two different innovation proxies. The trade performances of Belgium, Italy and Denmark are all significantly related to relative innovation using the *RTA* proxy, but not with the difference in per capita patents.

Looking more closely at the data it is clear that the ratio of per capita patents varies considerably, for instance in one sector Belgium has one patent, and Germany has 52. Removing one outlier in the case of both Belgium and

Denmark leads to a significant relationship between *PAT* and trade performance. Small countries, which have highly specialized innovation patterns such as Belgium and Denmark, have higher per capita patents than Germany in some sectors, and almost none in others, and as a result the *PAT* index is highly volatile.

Table 4.6 Bilateral flows with respect to West Germany

Proxy	RTA			PAT		
	α	INN	R^2 F	α	INN	R^2 F
Bel.	0.19	0.74**	0.14	0.14	0.01	0.02
	(0.05)	(0.29)	6.37**	(0.07)	(0.01)	0.63
Italy	0.19	0.74**	0.09	0.06	0.02	0.06
	(0.05)	(0.37)	3.91**	(0.09)	(0.02)	2.32
Ireland	0.05	0.22	0.01	0.10	−0.01	0.01
	(0.08)	(0.37)	0.34	(0.11)	(0.01)	0.28
Den.	0.37	0.70***	0.19	0.30	0.02	0.03
	(0.05)	(0.23)	9.14***	(0.08)	(0.02)	1.35
Port.	0.57	−0.02	0.00	0.61	−0.001	0.02
	(0.08)	(0.25)	0.01	(0.09)	(0.001)	0.79
Spain	0.41	−0.24	0.03	0.38	0.001	0.01
	(0.06)	(0.23)	1.07	(0.09)	(0.002)	0.37
UK	0.32	0.001	0.00	0.32	0.001	0.00
	(0.05)	(0.57)	0.00	(0.14)	(0.05)	0.00
France	0.21	0.79***	0.20	−0.02	0.11***	0.21
	(0.04)	(0.26)	9.34***	0.08)	(0.03)	10.3***
NL	0.24	0.48**	0.10	0.15	0.02*	0.08
	(0.06)	(0.24)	4.19**	(0.07)	(0.01)	3.28*
All	0.28	0.32***	0.03	0.26	0.002**	0.01
	(0.02)	(0.09)	10.6***	(0.02)	(0.001)	4.95**
More dev.	0.25	0.66***	0.12	0.19	0.02**	0.03
	(0.03)	(0.12)	31.8***	(0.03)	(0.01)	6.01**
Less dev.	0.35	−0.01	0.00	0.32	0.001	0.01
	(0.05)	(0.17)	0.00	(0.05)	(0.001)	0.84

Notes
*** *t*-statistic significant at 1%, ** significant at 5%, * significant at 10%.

Given the different specifications of the patent proxies, with the *RTA* index giving an indication of technological specialization rather than absolute advantage, it appears that Belgium, Italy and Denmark have a positive relationship between their pattern of innovation and their bilateral trade performance with Germany.

For the less-developed European countries in the sample (Ireland, Portugal and Spain) trade with Germany does not seem to be influenced by their relative innovation patterns with Germany, or by their innovation specialization. It is interesting to note that the UK has results consistent with the less-developed countries in the sample.

There appears to be a division between the more-developed and less-developed countries in the sample. This separation into two groups: developed countries – France, Belgium, Italy, Denmark, the UK, France and the Netherlands – and less-developed countries – Spain, Portugal and Ireland – was tested relative to the countries pooled together in one group. The pooled model estimating all the countries' trade flows together was rejected against separating the trade flows into those with developed and developing countries using an F-test. The results for the two different groups are presented in the last three rows of Table 4.6.

The results confirm that relative innovation is more important in explaining trade performance among the more-developed countries than it is between Germany and the three less-developed countries, namely Ireland, Spain and Portugal. The difference between the two groups is more marked using the RTA index than patent differences, as noted earlier; although for both groups the pooling is rejected. Ireland may be a special case, because of the importance of MNCs in Ireland in sectors such as chemicals. Ireland is also a location point for assembling products largely produced abroad, with government incentives given to MNCs to locate there. As a result, the impact of indigenous Irish innovation (shown by the number of Irish patents) is unlikely to be related to its trade performance in many key sectors dominated by foreign direct investment. However, despite this specific explanation in the case of Ireland, it may also be the case that relative innovation patterns are more important in influencing trade between the more advanced countries in Europe. This is consistent with the original Posner theory, which postulated differences in innovation as a motivation for trade between countries with similar endowments.

This subsection has concentrated on the results for the bilateral flows considered, and pooled by the country of origin; the next one gives some results for the relationship between relative innovation and trade performance on a sector basis.

4.2.4 An Analysis by Sector

In order to have enough data points to estimate the model separately for each sector, the six bilateral flows between the four European countries used earlier are pooled together for all three years, 1979, 1983 and 1987. There is a great deal of heterogeneity between the forty sectors; they vary from very-high-technology industries – such as computers and electronics – to resource-based industries such as food and petroleum. *A priori* we expect considerable variation in the relationship between relative innovation and trade performance according to the sector being considered. While differences in innovation may be an important source of trade in some sectors, trade in other sectors is motivated by factors such as the availability of natural resources, capital or cheap labour. The impact of these additional factors will be considered in Chapter 5. The relationship is estimated using differences in patents (PAT) as the explanatory variable, the difference in revealed technological advantage is not used, as the *RTA* index weights innovation differences by the overall proportion of patents, and therefore includes inter-industry variations in patenting performance. This makes it less appropriate for models estimated by sector. The influence of the size of the economy is taken care of in the use of trade performance as the dependent variable, and relative patents per capita as the explanatory variable. The results are given in Table 4.7 for all forty sectors.

For exactly half of the sectors, the correlation between trade performance and relative innovation is positive and significant. These sectors include the majority of the very-high-technology sectors and all but three of the medium-high technology sectors (see the Appendix).[11] It is noticeable that for the medium-low technology sectors only one correlation (textile products) is positively significant. In five cases, contrary to expectations, the relationship is negatively significant; in addition, two of these cases are very-high-technology sectors (agricultural chemicals and electronics), while the other three are classified as medium-low-technology sectors. For the remaining 15 sectors the relationship is not significant; in the majority of cases (nine) the relationship is positive, while in the other six cases it is negative.

The explanatory power of the correlation varies considerably from sector to sector. In five sectors it is very high (about 70 per cent or more). These are medium-high-technology sectors, particularly the machinery sectors (textile machinery has the highest explanatory power); other sectors are metal-working machinery, engines and turbines, fabricated metal products and electrical industrial appliances. In the case of these sectors, differences in innovation appear to be strongly correlated with trade performance, confirming earlier results by Soete (1981, 1987) and Fagerberg (1994b).

Table 4.7 Correlations by sector

Sector	α	PAT	R^2/F
Pharmaceuticals	−0.09	0.16**	0.21
	(0.07)	(0.08)	4.17**
Agricultural chemicals	0.66	−0.64***	0.59
	(0.15)	(0.13)	22.8***
Office and computers	−0.17	0.05	0.08
	(0.05)	(0.04)	1.36
Electronics	0.61	−0.54***	0.50
	(0.19)	(0.13)	16.1***
Aircraft	−0.25	0.11**	0.26
	(0.10)	(0.05)	5.71**
Arms	−0.54	0.23***	0.53
	(0.17)	(0.05)	18.1***
Inorganic chemicals	−0.13	0.20**	0.19
	(0.15)	(0.10)	3.84*
Plastics and synthetics	−0.29	0.21***	0.36
	(0.13)	(0.07)	8.92***
Paints	−0.41	0.17***	0.32
	(0.08)	(0.06)	7.65***
Other chemicals	−0.16	0.17**	0.23
	(0.09)	(0.07)	4.90**
Fabricated metal	−0.49	0.44***	0.69
	(0.08)	(0.07)	34.9***
Engines, turbines	−0.45	0.35***	0.73
	(0.07)	(0.05)	42.7***
Construction machinery	−0.54	0.47***	0.20
	(0.11)	(0.10)	19.7***
Metal-working machinery	−0.51	0.27***	0.74
	(0.07)	(0.40)	45.2***
Textile machinery	−0.56	0.31***	0.81
	(0.06)	(0.04)	65.0***
Refrigeration	0.06	−0.12	0.10
	(0.11)	(0.09)	1.79
Other non-electrical machinery	−0.26	0.11**	0.21
	(0.08)	(0.05)	4.24**
Electrical equipment	−0.48	0.33***	0.55
	(0.09)	(0.07)	19.8***
Electrical industrial appliances	−0.39	0.29***	0.69
	(0.06)	(0.05)	35.4***
Household appliances	−0.31	0.24***	0.41
	(0.13)	(0.07)	11.2***
Lighting	−0.38	0.20	0.08
	(0.22)	(0.17)	1.37

Sector	α	PAT	R^2/F
Radio and TV	−0.05	−0.07	0.04
	(0.15)	(0.08)	0.71
Other electrical	−0.20	0.23**	0.22
	(0.14)	(0.11)	4.56**
Motor vehicles	−0.28	0.32***	0.49
	(0.14)	(0.08)	15.6***
Instruments	−0.37	0.20***	0.46
	(0.06)	(0.05)	13.8***
Petroleum	−0.17	−0.09	0.01
	(0.27)	(0.06)	0.03
Food	−0.03	0.06	0.09
	(0.13)	(0.05)	1.63
Textile products	−0.13	0.05*	0.15
	(0.13)	(0.03)	2.93*
Soaps etc.	0.14	−0.08*	0.19
	(0.12)	(0.04)	3.85*
Organic chemicals	−0.14	0.01	0.11
	(0.05)	(0.01)	2.12
Rubber	0.22	−0.06*	0.17
	(0.11)	(0.03)	3.39*
Stone, clay, glass	−0.04	0.01	0.01
	(0.15)	(0.04)	0.08
Primary ferrous products	0.24	−0.07	0.08
	(0.14)	(0.06)	1.34
Non-ferrous metals	−0.13	0.02	0.13
	(0.12)	(0.04)	0.22
Farm machinery	−0.34	0.11	0.13
	(0.21)	(0.07)	2.30
General industrial machinery	−0.06	−0.03	0.01
	(0.18)	(0.06)	0.20
Ships etc.	0.22	0.05	0.06
	(0.13)	(0.05)	1.11
Railroad equipment	−0.07	0.08	0.06
	(0.27)	(0.08)	0.96
Motorcycles	0.43	−0.10**	0.23
	(0.17)	(0.05)	4.70**
Other transport	0.09	−0.07	0.05
	(0.22)	(0.07)	0.90

Notes:
*** *t*-statistic significant at 1%, ** significant at 5%, * significant at 1%.

These sectors have been termed 'production intensive' sectors by Pavitt (1984), based on the characteristics of their innovation pattern. The machinery sectors are high producers of innovations and constitute a vital source of innovations used in other sectors. As many of these innovations occur as a result of the production process, rather than through formal R&D, patents are better at capturing the innovation output from these sectors than a proxy based on R&D expenditure would have been.

For a second group of sectors, differences in innovation explain about 50 per cent of the variance in trade performance; these sectors are instruments, motor vehicles, armaments and electrical equipment, which include some very-high- and other medium-high-technology sectors. Within the very-high-technology sectors in general, the correlations results are mixed. It is surprising to note that both the high-technology sectors which are considered protected (armaments and aircraft) show a positive relationship between the patenting index and trade performance, despite the desire for secrecy impeding patents and the poor correlation in the case of the UK in Subsection 4.2.2. In two sectors there are negative and highly significant relationships, and for a third (computers) there is a positive but insignificant relationship. One explanation for these poor results is that there is a large amount of free riding in these sectors on other firms' innovations and, as a result, patents may not be a good indicator for technological capabilities. This is particularly the case for the computing sector, which may not want to disclose the technical information required when taking out a patent, because of the potential for 'cloning' within the industry.

Regarding the negative relationship for agricultural chemicals, this result is influenced by the bilateral flows between France and the Netherlands and the UK and Germany, which show a consistently negative relationship between relative innovation and trade performance. Germany took out the most patents in this sector, followed by the UK, but Germany is a net importer of agricultural chemicals from the UK, despite its higher level of patenting. In addition, France, which produces many more patents per capita in this sector than the Netherlands, has a negative trade balance with them for all three years. These apparently perverse bilateral relationships contribute to the negative relationship found in this sector between relative innovation and trade performance, which is true for both the French–Dutch and German–British relationships. This is perhaps indicative of specialization within the sector; for instance, the UK and Germany are specialized in different areas of agricultural chemicals. In addition, MNCs are important producers in this sector; they may undertake foreign direct investment rather than exports, and as a result the export pattern will not match the high level of patents. Patel and Pavitt (1991) estimate that 79 per cent of patents taken out in the US in agricultural chemicals for the period 1981–86 come from the 92 of the world's largest 686 firms which are active in this sector. This high concentration indicates the domination of the global market by a small number of very large firms, and, assuming that the majority of these large firms are MNCs, points to an important role for foreign direct investment in this sector.

The results of this subsection are broadly similar to those found by Soete (1981, 1987) and Dosi et al. (1990), with many medium-high-technology sectors such as the machinery sectors, engines and turbines, and the chemical industries showing a positive relationship between innovation and trade performance, as well as some very-high-technology sectors. However, in his model for a larger sample of countries, using the share of exports in the OECD as the dependent variable, and including the capital to labour ratio, population and a distance variable as additional explanatory variables, Soete found a positive and significant coefficient on the patent variable for both the electronics and the computer and office machinery sectors, and a positive but insignificant relationship for agricultural chemicals. Using exports per capita all the relationships with patenting were positive but none of them was significant for these sectors. The different results for these important industries may reflect differences in the sample of countries chosen (four EU countries against the OECD countries), or the influence of the other explanatory variables in the model.

Fagerberg (1994b) considered the relationship between country-level variables including R&D as a proportion of trade, population, the wage rate and investment for 19 OECD countries, and their specialization pattern shown by the revealed comparative advantage index. As in the results presented here he found no relationship between a patent variable and specialization for either the computer or the electronics sector. However, when substituting an R&D variable for the patent variable he did find a positive and significant relationship between R&D expenditure and a specialization in electronics, although not for computers. These results indicate that the inclusion of additional countries and explanatory variables may not change the results for these key sectors, but rather it is the choice of proxy which is important in influencing the results. There is some evidence (Grupp, 1991; Engelsman and van Raan, 1990) that international trade in high-technology goods is less influenced by innovation (as shown by patents) than other goods. One reason is that some very-high-technology sectors are dominated by military spending, so strategic interests may reduce the level of patenting. Another is a general desire for secrecy; in sectors in which changes in technology are of vital importance there is an even greater incentive to protect that innovation from imitation, which may be better served by secrecy than by patenting.

To summarize, the sector-level results show considerable variations in the relationship between relative innovation and bilateral trade performance on a sectoral basis. While for some sectors differences in innovation are strongly correlated with trade performance, for others there is no significant relationship between the two.

4.3 CONCLUSIONS

These four European countries were chosen in order to test the technology gap theory for countries at a similar stage of development. The countries in this sample are important trading partners for each others' goods and are highly integrated economically. The first set of results, considering the relationship between sector- and country-specific differences in innovation and bilateral trade performance, highlighted important differences between the countries. Including all forty sectors in the estimation and considering only the bilateral flows between the four countries, France and Germany appear to have their bilateral trade performances influenced by relative innovation. Taking European trade in general, with a multilateral export share dependent variable, the Netherlands is also influenced by relative innovation. Finally, once the two sectors of petroleum and armaments are taken out (as for particular reasons they do not appear to be influenced by relative innovation), the UK export share in Europe also appears to be influenced by differences in innovation.

These results indicate that even for this group of similar and economically integrated countries, differences in innovation levels continue to exist among them and provide an important determinant for differences in bilateral trade performance. The competitive advantage which results from differences in innovation appears to remain specific to a sector within a country in a number of cases. This supports the notion of national systems of innovation: some countries have areas of strength based on individual innovation patterns, institutions and economic structure, which have an impact on trade performance and can be maintained over time. These technology gaps can persist despite economic integration, strong trading links, and important cross-border direct investment between countries.

As the UK results show, there is a large degree of diversity between the different sectors. As a result the model was re-estimated for each individual sector. Twenty of the sectors show positive and significant correlations between innovation and trade performance, mainly in the very-high- and medium-high-technology sectors. For a number of high-technology sectors (agricultural chemicals, electronics and computers) the correlations were either negative, or not significant, possibly indicating drawbacks in the proxy; other results have shown positive relationships for those sectors when substituting R&D intensity for patents. Overall, the results confirm the impact of innovation on trade performance; as well as the variation in the relationship over sectors. For some of the sectors, relative innovation appears to be the *major* factor influencing bilateral trade performance between the European countries, for others it explains a significant part of trade performance, while for some sectors it plays a relatively minor role.

The results presented in this chapter are of a preliminary nature; the exclusion of other potentially important factors, such as the capital to labour ratio, may be a source of bias. However, the model is estimated at a detailed sectoral level, covering a broad range of sectors. In addition, two patent-based proxies are used, and account is taken of the size of the country when making the innovation proxy. In order to take account of the influence of factors other than innovation on trade performance a more fully specified model of the relationship between trade and innovation is considered for the OECD countries in the chapter which follows.

The variation in attitudes to innovation shown by the European countries, and the impact this has on their trade performance, implies a lack of 'real' convergence between European countries. Differences in innovation are one cause of differences in competitiveness and hence market shares. This chapter has considered technology gaps within a static framework, but other studies, outlined in Chapter 2, show that differences in innovation also have an important impact on the long-run competitiveness of advanced countries. Differences in innovation can also affect growth rates, which provides a potential source of divergence among countries. If different European countries are characterized by varying levels of innovation, this may affect not just their trade specialization and competitiveness, but also their level of employment and growth rates. In terms of policy, the significance of patterns of innovation within Europe has been partly acknowledged, and there are a number of projects aimed at building a joint European pattern of innovation, through private joint agreements and through the policies of the European Commission. However, in general the discussion of convergence within Europe has focused on the convergence of monetary variables – such as the level of public deficit and the rate of inflation – rather than on the convergence of 'real' variables, including the level of innovation. Nevertheless it appears that differences in innovation, or technology gaps, are an important determining factor of intra-European trade flows, even among the more advanced countries within the EU.

NOTES

1. For a study of the employment effects of differences in competitiveness for three European countries, see Verspagen and Wakelin (1997b).
2. There are a number of surveys on the use of patents as indicators. See, for instance, Basberg (1987), Pavitt (1985) and Soete and Wyatt (1983).
3. The OECD (1986) contains a statistical test based on the proportion of patents granted to foreign and domestic applications. It concluded that this was higher for foreign applications implying that they were on average of 'better quality' than the domestic applications.
4. There may be an Anglophone bias in using US data which favours those countries with close cultural and trading links with the US, for example, the UK in this sample. Archibugi and Pianta (1992) show how the pattern of patenting can vary according to the patenting institution chosen. Another problem, that of how to correct the bias of being the home country, does not arise as the US is not included in the sample.
5. There is also the problem of reclassifying the data from a technical to an industrial classification in order to make them comparable, see Pavitt (1985). The data used in this chapter have been reclassified by Engelsman and van Raan (1990) to a SIC classification.
6. Patents can be weighted by the citation counts in order to control for quality, see Henderson et al. (1992).
7. Correlations were also made for 1983; as there are no substantial differences in the results, only those for 1987 are presented.
8. The trade data come from Eurostat and were reclassified from the Standard International Trade Classification (SITC) revision 2 to the Standard Industrial Classification (SIC); see the Appendix.
9. This was introduced by Soete (1981) and is analogous to Balassa's revealed comparative advantage index. It should be noted that the index is not symmetrical. Attempts have been made to improve the index, for example, Engelsman and van Raan (1990) use the log value; the calculations here were repeated with the log index and the results were unchanged.
10. The dependent variable was also rescaled to take account of the EU's trade performance with the rest of the world. The results are consistent with those already presented and are not given here.
11. Using the OECD classification based on the R&D intensity of the production of OECD countries weighted by their contribution to total OECD production, discussed in Engelsman and van Raan (1990). It disguises some variations in R&D intensity between different countries within each sector, and as a result should only be used as a guideline. The last group includes both low-technology and medium-technology sectors because of difficulties in separating these groups, while the high-technology sectors have been separated into very-high-technology and medium-high-technology sectors.

APPENDIX TO 4A

Table 4A.1   The concordance between the Standard International Trade Classification (SITC Rev.2) and the US Standard Industrial Classification (SIC)

Sector	SIC	SITC Revised 2
Very-high-technology		
1. Pharmaceutics	283	541 (541.9)
2. Agricultural chemicals	287	562 (562.3)
3. Office, computing and accounting Machines	357	751.1, 751.2, 752, 751.81, 751.88, 759.11, 759.15, 759.9, 745.25, 745.26
4. Communication equipment, electronic components	366, 367	764.1, 764.2, 764.91, 764.92, 776, 778.85, 898.3
Protected very-high-technology		
5. Aircrafts and parts	372	713.1, 714.4, 714.81, 714.91, 718.88, 792 (792.83)
6. Ordnance (arms), space vehicles and parts	376, 348, 3795	894.6, 951
Medium-high-technology		
7. Inorganic chemistry	281	287.32, 323.21, 522, 523, 524, 533.1, 562.3
8. Plastic materials and synthetic resins	282	233.1, 266, 267, 582, 583, 585
9. Paints and allied products	285	533.4, 533.5
10. Other chemicals	289	572, 592, 598.2, 598.3, 598.9, 533.2, 551.30a
11. Fabricated metal products	34 (3462, 3463, 348)	69 (697.35, 697.51, 697.81), 711, 718.7, 741 (741.31), 749.2, 812.1, 697.51
12. Engines, turbines	351	712, 713 (713.1), 714.88, 718.8 (718.88)
13. Construction material, machinery	353	723, 728.3, 728.41, 744, 782.2
14. Metal-working machinery and equipment	354	736, 737 (737.32), 728.1, 745.1, 749.91, 695.4

Sector	SIC	SITC Revised 2
15. Textile, paper and printing machinery	355	724, 725, 726, 727, 775.12, 723.48, 728.42, 728.49, 741.6
16. Refrigeration	358	741.4, 741.5
17. Other nonelectrical machinery	359	714.99, 749.99, 699.61
18. Electrical transmission and distribution equipment	361, 3825	772, 874.8, 873.1
19. Electrical industrial apparatus	362	716, 771, 778.8 (778.85), 737.32, 741.31
20. Household appliances	363	775 (775.12, 775.3), 724.3
21. Electrical lighting and wiring equipment	364	778.2, 812.42, 812.43
22. Radio and television	365	761, 762, 763, 764 (764.91, 764.92)
23. Other electrical equipment	369	774, 778.1, 778.3
24. Motor vehicles and equipment	371	781, 783, 782.1, 784.1, 784.9
25. Professional and scientific instruments	38 (3825)	541.9, 751.82, 759.19, 871, 872, 873, 874 (874.8), 881, 882, 884, 885
Medium-low-technology		
26. Petroleum, natural gas, extraction and refining	13, 29	333, 334, 335 (335.2), 341.3, 341.4
27. Food and kindred Products	20	01, 02, 03, 042, 046, 047, 048, 056, 057.52, 057.6, 057.99, 057.96, 057.97, 058, 061.2, 061.5, 061.9, 062, 071, 072.2, 073, 074, 075, 081.2, 09, 11, 211, 4
28. Textile mill products	22	651 (651.95, 651.21), 652, 653, 654, 655, 656, 657, 659 (659.70a), 847.22
29. Soaps, cleaners, toilet goods	284	553.00b, 554
30. Organic chemistry	286	51, 335.2, 531, 532, 551.30, 551.4, 553.00a, 598.1
31. Rubber, miscellaneous plastic products	30	62, 848.22, 848.21, 584

Sector	SIC	SITC Revised 2
32. Stone, clay, glass and concrete products	32	66 (667), 812.2, 651.95, 773.2, 812.41
33. Primary ferrous products	331, 332, 3399, 3462	67, 694.01, 694.03a
34. Primary and secondary non–ferrous metals	333–336, 3398, 3463	68 (686.32, 689.14), 773.1
35. Farm and garden machinery and equipment	352	721
36. General industrial machinery	356	741.1, 741.32, 742, 743, 749.1, 749.3
37. Ship, boat building, repairs	373	793
38. Railroad equipment	374	791, 786.13
39. Motorcycles, bicycles and parts	375	785.1, 785.39a, 785.2
40. Miscellaneous transportation equipment	379 (3795)	786.11, 786.12, 786.8

Note: Industries in parentheses are not included in the aggregate.

5. The Impact of Innovation on Bilateral OECD Trade

There is a growing literature estimating the empirical determinants of trade, either for one country, frequently the United States, or for a group of countries such as the OECD. This chapter considers the bilateral trade flows of nine OECD countries, all advanced industrialized countries and important trading partners. Taking the bilateral flows of nine industrialized countries reduces the universality of the results, but makes the estimation of the determinants of trade more feasible. We expect differences in innovation to be one of the key determinants of bilateral trade performance between these countries.

This chapter extends the previous one by considering the impact of innovation on trade for a wider selection of countries. Whereas the previous chapter examined simple correlations between innovation patterns and export performance, in this chapter factors in addition to innovation (relative wage costs and investment rates) are included in the model. One drawback of the more complete data set is some loss in detail: data for only 22 sectors are available, unlike the 40 considered in the previous chapter. The inclusion of additional explanations for trade performance is important, as no one theory of trade can explain trade performance in all sectors. As Vernon (1966, p. 198) put it: 'in an area as complex and "imperfect" as international trade and investment, however, one ought not anticipate that any hypothesis will have more than a limited explanatory power'.

The aim of the chapter is to assess the importance of differences in innovation in influencing the bilateral trade performance of the countries in the sample. Three out of the four countries already analysed are included (the Netherlands is not) and in addition three are other advanced European countries – Norway, Sweden and Italy – as well as Canada, Japan and the US. This larger selection of countries encompasses a greater proportion of world trade, including the important bilateral relations between Japan and the US, and Japan and Europe. These trade relations have been the subject of much recent discussion, particularly in terms of a loss of competitiveness of both the US and Europe with respect to Japan. Innovation is seen as a key feature in explaining Japan's competitiveness in world trade, and observers in both the US (see, for instance, Tyson, 1992) and Europe (Freeman et al., 1991), show concern that both are 'falling behind' with respect to Japan.

There are three issues concerning the relationship between innovation and trade performance which this chapter wishes to address. The first is to assess how the trade performance relationship varies over countries and industries. In order to investigate this, dummy variables are included both for the sector and for the country of origin to control for the influence of factors which vary across sectors for a particular country, and across countries for a particular sector. The second issue is to evaluate the impact of a change of innovation proxy on the results. As it is difficult to capture all the aspects of the innovation process in one proxy, the use of different technology proxies may highlight diverse aspects of technology. As a result a number of proxies are used in this chapter: relative R&D intensity, relative patenting in the US and the number of innovations used and produced in the UK.

Third, the impact on trade performance of being a net user or net producer of innovations is examined. There are some sectors in the economy which are characterized by high levels of innovation (such as the machinery sectors), while other sectors produce few innovations, but use innovations produced in different sectors, for instance from sectors which supply them with inputs. The general proxies for innovation, such as patents and R&D expenditure, cannot capture this diffusion of innovation from one sector to another. The actual counts of innovation used in this chapter are classified both by the sector that produced them and by the sector that first used them. This is used to assess the impact being either a net user or net producer has on trade performance, and how the impact of R&D expenditure on trade performance varies for these two groups of sectors. The division of sectors into net users and net producers of innovations may be more informative then alternative separations based on, for instance, R&D intensity.

The chapter is set out as follows. The first section presents an outline of the recent experience of this sample of OECD countries in terms of economic convergence. The second section sets out the empirical model used; and the third presents the results. The results are largely consistent with expectations: the investment and innovation variables are positively significant and the labour coefficient is negatively significant; there is considerable heterogeneity across sectors and countries. In Section 4 the problem of a proxy for innovation is outlined and the model is re-estimated substituting a patent index for relative R&D intensity as the innovation variable. In order to analyse the relationship between the proxies, survey data from the SPRU survey of major UK innovations is introduced, and the relationship between the patent index, R&D intensity and innovations is considered for the UK.

The last part of the section re-estimates the model only for the UK using innovation count. The results are different when considering gross exports rather than net trade; the former is taken as more appropriate for use with the innovation variables which reflect only UK innovation. Section 5 separates industries by the ratio between innovations used and produced in each. When the model is estimated separately for each group, this separation is accepted for the full sample of OECD countries and for the subsample of UK bilateral trade flows. R&D expenditure and investment have more impact on trade performance for the producers of technology than for the users. Finally, Section 6 gives some conclusions.

5.1 CONVERGENCE AMONG THE OECD COUNTRIES

Technology gaps have important implications for the economic convergence of countries in terms of their development. As innovation is a key factor affecting growth rates, international differences in innovation (technology gaps) are one explanation for international variations in growth rates. The logic is that being on the technological frontier leads to greater competitiveness and a higher standard of living; however, technologically less-advanced countries can imitate new technologies at low costs, and converge to the higher-income level at the technological frontier.[1] The diffusion process thus provides the potential for 'catching-up' to the more advanced countries; how automatic this catching-up process is in practice has the been the subject of much discussion (see, for instance Abromovitz, 1986 and Baumol, 1986). The potential to assimilate technological knowledge may require some basic capabilities, without which knowledge-spillovers do not occur. For instance, empirical studies have pointed to the importance of the level of education of the workforce (Baumol et al., 1989), as affecting a country's ability to catch up.

Considering the cumulative and path-dependent nature of much technological change, many observers (see, for instance, Dosi et al., 1990) have suggested that technology gaps may continue over time, even in the same products and sectors, without the technology automatically being diffused to other countries. Innovations can be partly appropriated at the firm and country level, so that any country is constrained by its current technological capabilities and its structure and pattern of specialization (Lundvall, 1992). In this sense, a country's pattern of trade, and hence specialization can have repercussions for its ability to either converge or diverge. In keeping with both a neo-Schumpeterian perspective and international growth models (Grossman and Helpman, 1991) endogenous comparative advantage and technology mean that international trade is an important influence on a country's pattern of growth. As a result, the existence of technology gaps which influence trade can have an important impact on a country's trade performance, but also on a country's growth experience.[2]

The OECD countries are generally considered to have seen a period of convergence in the post-war period, particularly in the 1960s and 1970s, when Europe and Japan closed the gap with the United States (Maddison, 1991). In order to consider the recent experience of the nine countries of this sample, coefficients of variation were calculated for a number of macroeconomic variables. The countries in the sample – Canada, France, Germany, Italy, Japan, Norway, Sweden, the UK and the US – are all advanced industrialized countries, many of which are on the technological frontier in at least some sectors. The others should have no impediment to assimilating knowledge via spillovers, thus we would expect to see convergence over the period. The coefficients are taken as the standard deviation over the mean for each of six variables across the nine countries for five separate years between 1970 and 1989 and are presented in Table 5.1. A fall in the coefficient indicates convergence, or a lower dispersal of the sample countries around the mean, likewise a rise in the coefficient indicates divergence.

Table 5.1 Coefficients of variation (standard deviation/mean) for the sample countries

Variable	1970	1975	1980	1985	1989
GDP per capita (US$ PPP)	0.21	0.17	0.15	0.14	0.14
Wage rate (US$)	0.40	0.23	0.18	0.25	0.11
Manufacturing labour productivity	0.20	0.18	0.21	0.21	0.28
Manufacturing unit wage costs	0.20	0.14	0.16	0.13	0.13
Gross investment / GDP (US$ PPP)	0.23	0.33	0.23	0.21	0.24*
Business R&D / GDP (US$ PPP)**	–	0.42	0.47	0.46	0.46

Notes:
* Excluding Italy; ** only for business expenditure on R&D in manufacturing sectors.

Source: OECD International Sectoral Database, and OECD STAN database.

For the period 1970–89 a clear pattern of convergence emerges, GDP per capita among the countries converges, especially in the first five years, after which the level of dispersal is stable; manufacturing unit wage costs show a similar pattern. The wage rate is more volatile, showing convergence until 1980 and then divergence and finally considerable convergence from 1985 to 1989. In contrast, it is in the final period that productivity levels in manufacturing appear to diverge after being stable in the earlier periods. For the investment variable divergence occurs until 1975 after which there is a period of convergence and then again divergence. Business R&D expenditure as a proportion of GDP shows no convergence; there is some indication of divergence from 1975–80 and then stability.

This preliminary evidence indicates that the process of convergence among the OECD countries considered here does appear to have been active in the last 20 years in terms of GDP per capita, labour productivity and unit labour costs. Other indicators show some divergence, namely productivity, the investment rate and the proportion of GDP spent on R&D, all of which show more dispersal at the end of the period than at the beginning. The wage rate shows considerable volatility over the period but the coefficient of variation finishes at a much lower level in 1989 than in 1970. It is worth noting that the proportion of GDP spent on R&D shows no convergence over the period, and has the highest coefficient of variation of all the variables considered, noticeably more than either gross investment or wage costs. Thus it appears that in terms of resources committed to R&D the countries in the sample still show considerable heterogeneity. The analysis which follows attempts to estimate the importance of differences in innovation in influencing trade performance for these countries. The relationship is considered on a static basis for the 1980s, which appears to have been a period of relative stability in terms of convergence for these countries.[3]

5.2 AN EMPIRICAL MODEL OF TRADE AND INNOVATION

The hypothesis to be tested is the role of differences in innovation in explaining bilateral trade performance. The model is static and uses international data, considering *relative* innovation, labour costs and investment rates as sources of competitiveness, and hence trade. Following the technology gap theory we expect relative R&D intensity to be positively related to export performance for a number of reasons. High R&D intensity both introduces new products to the market, and raises the quality of existing goods which improves trade performance. In addition to product innovations and improvements, process innovation reduces costs and thus improves competitiveness. In keeping with the technology gap model, relative innovation is taken as the relevant explanatory variable.

Although technology is clearly an important factor in trade performance, other factors that influence trade performance also need to be taken into account. Indeed, investment is a complement to technological change as it increases the capacity and flexibility of production facilities, and adds to the quality of goods. As a result, a positive relationship is also expected between investment and trade performance.

The relative wage variable is included to capture cost differences between countries. In some models of trade performance relative prices have been used (Greenhalgh, 1990), while in others relative labour costs have been taken to reflect relative prices (Amable and Verspagen, 1995). However, the *a priori* expectations for the wage rate variable are potentially ambiguous. For sectors in which cost considerations are important, we would expect a lower wage rate to improve exports in that industry implying a negative sign on the coefficient. However, it is also possible that the wage rate variable acts as a proxy for the skill level of the economy (that is, countries with high wages often have a more skilled workforce), and as such it may have a positive relationship with trade performance. Other empirical studies, such as Fagerberg (1988), found trade performance to be more influenced by non-price factors, including innovation, than by cost competitiveness.

All the data used in this empirical model are on a country-specific and sector-specific basis for nine OECD countries and 22 manufacturing industries; the industries concerned are defined on the ISIC rev. 2 classification, under heading 3000; the sector definitions are given in the Appendix. The relationship estimated is given below:

$$\frac{X_{pqs}}{X_{qps}} = f[\ (\frac{W_{ps}}{W_{qs}}),\ (\frac{I_{ps}}{I_{qs}}),\ (\frac{K_{ps}}{K_{qs}})] \tag{5.1}$$

where the dependent variable is the ratio of exports from country p to country q over exports to q from p in sector s. This is on a bilateral basis for the nine countries which gives 36 bilateral flows. The explanatory variables are defined as follows:

W is the wage rate, defined as the wage bill over total employment, in a common currency; the wage variable given here is the relative wage rates for countries p and q in sector s;

K represents investment intensity, defined as gross fixed capital formation relative to production; the variable is the relative investment intensities between countries *p* and *q* in sector *s*;

I is the innovation variable which is proxied by either R&D expenditure or patents taken out in the US. These two variables are defined as:

> *R&D* – R&D intensity measured by R&D expenditure undertaken by business enterprises relative to production; the variable gives the relative R&D intensity between two countries *p* and *q* for sector *s*;
>
> *RTA* – the ratio of RTA indices[4] for countries *p* and *q* in sector *s*. The RTA index is given below where PAT are foreign patents taken out in the US; the index gives country *p*'s share of patents granted in the US in sector *s* over the country's total patent share.

$$RTA_{ps} = \frac{PAT_{ps} / \sum_p PAT_{ps}}{\sum_s PAT_{ps} / \sum_s \sum_p PAT_{ps}}$$

Attempts were also made with the patent intensity ratio used in the previous chapter, but problems of collinearity with both of the other explanatory variables meant it was dropped in favour of the RTA ratio. However, the drawbacks of such a ratio discussed in the earlier chapter should be kept in mind. Two technology variables are used as there are reasons to believe that innovation proxies, such as R&D intensity and patenting, may capture different aspects of the innovation process. Some industries may be R&D intensive but, for example, have a low output of patents for strategic reasons. Alternatively, innovations from small firms may generate patents, without having a formal R&D department, and of course there is a third category of innovations which neither result from a research programme and nor are they patented. The two proxies used in the first sections of this chapter show only one measurable input into the innovation process (R&D expenditure) and one measurable output (patents).

The relationship *f* is assumed to be linear. This relationship was examined pooled across nine OECD countries – Canada, France, Germany, the UK, Italy, Japan, Norway, Sweden, and the US – which gives 36 bilateral flows for 22 industries that is, 792 observations, although the existence of missing values lowers the number of observations.[5] The dependent variable is for 1988 and the explanatory variables are averages for 1980–88. The main reason for this is the practical one of smoothing the data for any variations in the explanatory variables which occur due to the business cycle.

5.3 THE RESULTS

5.3.1 The Pooled Results

Initially the relationship given in equation (5.1) was estimated according to equation (5.2) with all the data pooled; α is the intercept and ε is an error term. Following Davidson and MacKinnon (1981) a linear model was tested against a log-linear model and the latter was accepted as being more informative; as a result the log-linear model is used throughout.

$$\ln \frac{X_{pqs}}{X_{qps}} = \alpha + \beta_1 \ln(\frac{W_{ps}}{W_{qs}}) + \beta_2 \ln(\frac{I_{ps}}{I_{qs}}) + \beta_3 \ln(\frac{K_{ps}}{K_{qs}}) + \varepsilon \qquad (5.2)$$

Regressions were made using each of the innovation variables separately and estimated by OLS. The results for each regression are given in the first two rows of Table 5.2, with the standard errors in brackets.

Table 5.2 Pooled results

	α	K	W	I	R^2
RTA	−0.11	0.40***	−0.15***	0.35***	0.10
	(0.08)	(0.13)	(0.03)	(0.13)	
R&D	−0.12	0.75***	−0.15***	0.19***	0.11
	(0.07)	(0.12)	(0.03)	(0.06)	
Country dummies	–	0.70***	−0.13***	0.14**	0.17
		(0.13)	(0.03)	(0.07)	

Notes:
** Significant at 5%, *** at 1%.

The results are consistent with *a priori* expectations. The sign on the coefficient for the wage rate variable is negative (and significant), that is, as wage rates go up, trade performance worsens and there is no aggregate evidence for the skill hypothesis. For the investment variable there is a positive (and significant) relationship between investment and trade performance.[6] The two innovation variables considered separately are both positive and significant. These results indicate a definite role for innovation in influencing trade performance when considering the pooled data.

Although these results are consistent with expectations, they may disguise a great deal of variation both across sectors and countries. The pooled specification is restricted as it allows no variation in the relationship according to sector or country despite a large degree of diversity. The data set contains two dimensions over which it can be grouped; one is the 36 bilateral flows which can be assembled into eight groups according to the country of origin, the second is the 22 industries. By including dummies for the two groups – sectors and countries – the high degrees of freedom of a pooled model can be maintained. The dummies allow for variables that are constant either across sectors or across countries. A number of models are tested:

1. a restricted model pooling all the data;
2. a model including country dummies which allows the intercept to vary with the source country of each bilateral flow;
3. a model including sector dummies which allows the intercept to vary according to each sector;[7]
4. both sector and country fixed effects are included.

These models are estimated separately and then tested against each other. The pooled model given in the first line of Table 5.2 is taken as the restricted model; the R&D expenditure variable is used to include the maximum number of sectors as patent data are not available for three of the sectors. *F*-tests are made to test the inclusion of each set of dummies, the results of which are presented in Table 5.3. The *F*-tests show the importance of including country dummies in the analysis, while sector dummies were not significant. There is thus little evidence of factors which vary for each sector across countries. The two-way model with both country and industry dummies was not rejected relative to the pooled model, but an *F*-test for the joint country and sector model against the country model did not reject the country model, implying that the variation is mainly due to the country effects. As a result, the model including only country effects was taken as the most appropriate. The results with country dummies are given in the last row of Table 5.2.

As can be seen from Table 5.2, the results are not fundamentally altered by introducing country effects. The coefficient on the R&D variable changes from the pooled OLS model but remains positively significant at 5 per cent. Thus while there are significant country effects which need to be included, their inclusion does not appear to have any affect on the explanatory variables. Such effects may include structural variables referring to each country, such as the national system of innovation which are likely to vary considerably between countries (Chesnais, 1986).

Table 5.3 F-tests for the dummy variables

Test	Distribution	F-value	99% critical value
Country v. pooled	$F(7,491)$	4.94***	2.69
Sector v. pooled	$F(20,478)$	0.83	1.84
Country and sector v. pooled	$F(28,470)$	1.77***	1.74
Country and sector v. country	$F(21,470)$	0.73	1.84
Country and sector v. sector	$F(8,470)$	4.01***	2.55

Note: *** Significant at 1%.

Given that the impact of the explanatory variables may be over either countries or sectors, this is still a very restrictive specification and will lower the precision of the coefficients. The impact of specific industry or country effects on the explanatory variables, such as the high R&D intensity of specific countries or industries, cannot be assessed. There are economic reasons for believing that the impact of innovation on trade varies considerably over both these groups.

Countries have unique innovation profiles because of – among other factors – their historical development and their economic structure. As Archibugi and Pianta (1992) and Nelson (1993) have outlined, national technological profiles vary greatly, even among European countries, with each country having its strengths and weaknesses in innovation. This cross-country variation is to be expected as the countries in this sample vary considerably in their expenditure on R&D, education systems and emphasis on military or civilian research. Each individual industry will also have different characteristics which influence trade performance in the sector. Chapter 4 indicated the variation in the importance of the innovation variable over different sectors. As a result, it is necessary to consider a number of unrestricted models allowing the coefficients to vary across industries and countries.

5.3.2 Country and Sector Results

In order to maintain the maximum number of degrees of freedom, the data were considered separately on a country and an industry basis. For the first specification the bilateral data were grouped according to country of origin to give eight groups. The earlier results showed the importance of including intercept dummies for countries; in this model the explanatory variables were also allowed to vary according to country. The unrestricted model was not rejected at the 5 per cent level of significance with respect to that including only dummies, although it was rejected at 1 per cent. Overall, the homogeneity of the model given in Table 5.2 was rejected. The results are given in Table 5.4 with the standard errors in brackets.

Table 5.4 Country-specific results

Country	α	K	W	R&D
Canada	−0.73	1.43	−0.11	0.36
	(0.16)***	(0.27)***	(0.07)	(0.13)***
Germany	0.35	0.07	−0.09	0.12
	(0.14)***	(0.25)	(0.07)	(0.14)
France	0.25	0.57	−0.03	−0.07
	(0.28)	(0.37)	(0.12)	(0.23)
UK	−0.73	0.07	−0.23	0.14
	(0.31)**	(0.34)	(0.08)***	(0.15)
Italy	−1.32	0.75	−0.31	−0.27
	(0.62)**	(0.38)**	(0.14)**	(0.19)
Japan	0.74	1.97	−0.08	−0.21
	(0.47)	(0.52)***	(0.12)	(0.31)
Norway	−0.49	0.46	−0.24	0.27
	(0.39)	(0.61)	(0.13)**	(0.23)
Sweden	3.25	−4.26	0.25	0.88
	(2.55)	(3.83)	(0.49)	(1.03)

Notes:
$R^2 = 0.24$, ** significant at 5%, *** at 1%.

The results show considerable variation between countries, and illustrate the diversity that exists even among developed countries. The R&D variable is positive but not significant for four out of eight countries,[8] and positive and significant for Canada. It is negative but not significant for Italy, France and Japan. The labour variable coefficients are all negative with the exception of

Sweden, and significant in the case of the UK, Norway and Italy. For the investment variable all the coefficients are positive, again with the exception of Sweden, and are significant for Canada, Japan and Italy. These results both call into question the importance of technology on a country-by-country basis, and illustrate some variations between countries; the explanatory power has risen to 24 per cent, but remains low. Variations by country appear to take the form of jumps in the intercept rather than in variations in the coefficients on the explanatory variables. While a common intercept across the trade flows was rejected at 1 per cent, a common slope across the trade flows was not rejected at 1 per cent, but only at 5 per cent. National characteristics such as economic structure, institutions and government policy may be reflected in these fixed effects, which vary across all sectors for each individual country.

The model was then re-estimated on an industry basis. The model in Table 5.2, with R&D as the technology variable, was taken as the restricted model. A new specification was made with a single intercept but allowing the explanatory variables to vary with industries. The restricted pooled model was rejected relative to the unrestricted model, and overall homogeneity was rejected, implying important variations in the trade performance relationship over sectors. The results are presented in Table 5.5, with the standard errors given in brackets.

There are 12 out of the 22 industries which have positively significant coefficients on the R&D intensity variable. Only two of these, pharmaceuticals and aerospace, are considered very-high-technology industries using the OECD (1986) classification. Among the other industries for which the innovation variable is significant are medium-technology industries such as motor vehicles, fabricated metals, electrical and non-electrical machinery, ferrous and non-ferrous metals and paper and printing; this was also the case in the previous chapter.

There are also two low-technology industries: rubber and plastic, and stone, clay and glass, both of which could be considered natural resource industries. Thus it is not necessarily exclusively high-technology industries which invest in research in order to improve their trade performance; although not acting on the technological frontier, it appears that the benefits of research may be experienced in any manufacturing industry. Both the electronic and computer sectors have negative and significant coefficients on the technology variable; the coefficient for the oil-refining industry is also negative and significant. An insignificant long-run coefficient was found on the R&D variable for the electronics sector in Magnier and Toujas-Bernate (1994), indicating possible weaknesses in the innovation proxy. The R&D intensity variable

Table 5.5 Results by sector

	K	W	R&D
Aerospace	0.54	0.01	0.28*
	(0.97)	(0.11)	(0.15)
Chemicals	0.44	-0.12	0.72
	(1.39)	(0.13)	(0.87)
Pharmaceuticals	0.58	0.05	2.07***
	(0.78)	(0.11)	(0.57)
Oil refineries	-0.02	0.03	-0.86***
	(0.25)	(0.09)	(0.21)
Electronics	5.63***	-0.38***	-0.71*
	(1.96)	(0.11)	(0.40)
Electrical machinery	1.24	-0.41**	1.34***
	(1.29)	(0.18)	(0.47)
Instruments	0.18	-0.12	0.34
	(0.43)	(0.11)	(0.25)
Non-electrical machinery	2.72	-0.21*	1.83***
	(2.31)	(0.12)	(0.69)
Computers and office machinery	-2.70***	0.56***	-4.30***
	(0.65)	(0.18)	(1.01)
Food, drink	0.68	0.21***	-0.57**
	(0.85)	(0.08)	(0.24)
Rubber and plastic	0.26	-0.51***	1.35***
	(0.47)	(0.10)	(0.31)
Textiles	0.69	-0.30***	-0.39***
	(0.50)	(0.11)	(0.15)
Fabricated metal	0.40	-0.31***	1.22***
	(0.32)	(0.08)	(0.35)
Ferrous metals	0.24	-0.44***	1.21***
	(0.40)	(0.07)	(0.24)
Non-ferrous metals	1.26***	-0.07	0.88*
	(0.31)	(0.10)	(0.47)
Stone, clay, glass	1.92***	-0.39***	0.44**
	(0.67)	(0.09)	(0.20)
Other manufacturing	-1.63**	-0.29***	-1.40***
	(0.71)	(0.08)	(0.48)
Paper and printing	2.27***	0.08	0.48***
	(0.45)	(0.12)	(0.14)

	K	W	R&D
Wood	1.66***	0.17	0.61*
	(0.41)	(0.15)	(0.34)
Shipbuilding	−1.06	−0.14	0.55
	(2.38)	(0.60)	(0.45)
Motor vehicles	3.82***	−0.18	1.32**
	(1.52)	(0.13)	(0.70)

Notes:
$\alpha = -0.03$ (s.e. = 0.06), $R^2 = 0.53$, *** significant at 1%, ** at 5%, * at 10%.

may not capture all aspects of innovation as some innovative industries are not characterized by high R&D expenditure. For those which are, the inclusion of military research expenditure taking place in the private sector will alter the results. The efficiency of military R&D expenditure is lower as it is less likely to have economic spillovers than civilian-orientated research. Another problem with the results is the definitions of the industries used. In some cases – such as the important one of computers – low-technology products are also included in the definition of the industry. Thus the industry does not have coherent characteristics upon which it can be assessed. This also occurs within the electronics industry, which includes both semi-conductors and communication equipment, which incorporates products at different technology levels. For some products within the industry, innovation is still of primary importance and the industry is acting on the innovation frontier, while in others the products have become standardized and innovation is no longer of such importance. The impact of varying the proxy will be considered in the next section. The other drawback of the data, the generalised nature of the sector definitions, cannot be dealt with because of data limitations.

For the wage-cost variable we can examine the skill hypothesis; again on an individual industry basis. In two cases the wage-cost variable is positive and significant but the two industries, computers and food, have little in common. For the computing industry the skill hypothesis would seem feasible because of the technological sophistication of the product; however, a positive variable is not found for other high-technology industries such as aerospace or electronics. The labour-cost variable is generally negatively significant for medium-technology to low-technology sectors. The definitions of both industries in this sample are quite broad: the computing industry also includes office machinery while the food industry includes drink and tobacco. This diversity of products within many industries acts as an obstacle to obtaining clear results at a sector level. Nine industries have significant negative coefficients on the wage-cost variable; these include electronics, textiles, rubber, fabricated metals, ferrous metals, stone, clay and glass and other manufacturing. Trade performance in all these industries appears to be influenced by the availability of low-cost labour.

For the investment variable there are only six industries with a positive and significant coefficient and they are electronics, non-ferrous metals, stone and glass, paper and printing, motor vehicles and the wood sector – all medium-technology and low-technology sectors with the exception of electronics. The computing industry has a negatively significant coefficient which is contrary to expectations. There does not appear to be a clear response to investment based on the technology level of the industry; in general the coefficient has the expected sign so that investment intensity is positively related to trade performance for most industries, although the results are weak.

Although an exact comparison is impossible because of the different sectoral definitions, these results are broadly consistent with the results from the previous chapter. Electronics had a negative and significant sign also in these results, although the coefficient for computers was positive but not significant. There are other minor differences in some sectors such as textiles and rubber, but this could be partly due to differences in sector definitions, and the innovation proxy used.

5.4 SENSITIVITY ANALYSIS

5.4.1 The Patent Index

Although the choice of proxy did not influence the results using the pooled data (see Table 5.2), this may not be the case when considering industry-level data. Differences between two proxies such as R&D intensity and patents may be industry specific, with some industries investing heavily in research but not taking out patents for strategic reasons as they involve disclosing information. Alternatively, innovations may not occur because of research but rather as a result of learning by doing; such innovations can be patented but will not be captured by R&D statistics. This heterogeneity between different industries influences which innovation proxy is most appropriate. As a result, the model on a sector basis has been re-estimated using an alternative innovation proxy. The proxy used in this subsection is the difference in the RTA indices of the two countries involved in each bilateral flow.

Table 5.6 Results with patent index

	K	W	RTA
Aerospace	−0.70	−0.01	−1.28
	(0.73)	(0.12)	(0.95)
Chemicals	1.41	−0.02	2.35
	(1.51)	(0.14)	(1.67)
Pharmaceuticals	0.68**	0.31**	2.20***
	(0.87)	(0.14)	(0.62)
Oil refineries	0.24	−0.11	−0.03
	(0.32)	(0.10)	(0.42)
Electronics	3.10	−0.30**	1.03**
	(2.48)	(0.13)	(0.49)
Electrical machinery	1.18	−0.30	0.93*
	(1.59)	(0.20)	(0.49)
Instruments	0.06	−0.02	1.58***
	(0.40)	(0.12)	(0.63)
Non-electrical machinery	1.70	−0.20	−1.46
	(1.48)	(0.14)	(1.61)
Computers and office machinery	−0.25	−0.06	2.04***
	(0.55)	(0.12)	(0.64)
Food, drink	1.98**	0.23**	−0.01
	(0.82)	(0.12)	(0.52)
Rubber and plastic	0.31	−0.35***	3.90*
	(0.52)	(0.11)	(2.12)
Textiles	1.68***	−0.42***	0.72 ·
	(0.44)	(0.11)	(0.71)
Fabricated metal	0.86**	−0.07	−1.24**
	(0.40)	(0.13)	(0.61)
Ferrous metals	−0.38	−0.48***	1.64***
	(0.45)	(0.08)	(0.55)
Non-ferrous metals	1.21***	0.07	0.64
	(0.34)	(0.09)	(0.83)
Stone, clay, glass	2.57***	−0.20**	−2.80***
	(0.70)	(0.10)	(0.75)
Shipbuilding	−3.41***	−0.65***	−0.07
	(0.67)	(0.14)	(0.16)
Motor vehicles	2.18	−0.14	2.98***
	(1.53)	(0.10)	(0.78)

Notes: $\alpha = -0.17$** (s.e. = 0.07), $R^2 = 0.43$, *** significant at 1%, ** at 5%, * at 10%.

While the R&D variable shows absolute differences in technological capacity, the RTA index gives an indication of a country's comparative technological advantage. The RTA index reflects a country's relative strengths and weaknesses, and every country has a high RTA index in some industries even though it may not have an absolute technological advantage in them.[9] The results for the industry-level model are presented in Table 5.6 and are indeed substantially different from the earlier results.

The key high-technology industries of computers and electronics which had negatively significant coefficients with the R&D variable, now have positive and significant coefficients. In addition, the instruments sector has also become significant at 1 per cent. This may be due to the problems of appropriating the benefits of R&D expenditure in these sectors. Those countries which have produced patents and protected their innovations, benefit from them through improved export performance. This was not the case using a patent variable in Chapter 4; those results for these three sectors showed only instruments with a positive and significant coefficient. This may be due to using a different sample of countries, or the influence of the additional explanatory variables.

For a number of sectors, including non-electrical machinery, fabricated metals and aerospace, the patent variable is not significant when the R&D variable had been; some even become negative. The divergence between these and the earlier results implies that the two proxies reflect different aspects of the innovation process and this is shown up at the industry level; the majority of the industry coefficients change according to the proxy used. The patent proxy appears to capture innovation better than R&D expenditure in high-technology industries. Overall, for 15 out of the 22 sectors innovation had a positive and significant impact on bilateral trade performance with one or other of the proxies.

The other two variables also experience some changes. This appears to be due to collinearity between the R&D variable and the labour variable which are positively related and the R&D variable and the investment variable which are negatively related. The explanatory power falls considerably using patents as a substitute for R&D expenditure. Overall, the use of an alternative proxy for innovation has a definite impact on the results. For a number of industries – most notably high-technology industries – the results give a different characterization from the results using R&D intensity.

The next subsection uses a direct count of innovations to assess the impact of innovation on the trade of the UK.

5.4.2 Direct Innovation Counts

An alternative measure of innovation is available for the UK in the form of a survey of significant technical innovations undertaken by the Science Policy Research Unit (SPRU) at the University of Sussex. Significant innovations were defined as 'the successful commercial introduction of new or improved products, processes or materials' (p. 1 of Users' Manual), and as such can be differentiated from invention, the stage prior to economic implementation. They were identified by groups of experts and wherever possible the innovations were confirmed by the innovating firm itself. The survey is for the UK and covers more than 4,000 innovations for the period 1945 to 1983. Pavitt et al. (1987) and Robson et al. (1988), give details of the relationship between the production and use of innovations, and between process and product innovations, and about the survey in general. Two variables from the survey have been used in this subsection: the number of innovations being produced in an industry (defined using SIC 1968 at the four-digit level in the survey) and the number of innovations being used in that industry. These data were transformed using a correspondence to match the industries already used in this chapter (the details are in the Appendix). Four separate innovation variables were identified: the innovations used and produced in a sector for the entire period of the survey, and the innovations used and produced in a sector for the period 1979–83, that is, the last five years of the sample. The time period considered may alter the results; Greenhalgh (1990) found some evidence that the relationship between these innovation counts and trade performance alters with the time period considered, being significant only until the 1970s.

In order to analyse the interrelationships between the technology variables for the UK, the 22 sectors were considered on a sectoral basis and ranked according to their R&D expenditure (their cumulative expenditure on R&D from 1973 to 1990 termed *CUMRD*); the number of patents produced from 1973 to 1987 (termed *CUMPAT*); and the number of innovations produced from 1979 to 1983 (*PROD*) and the number of innovations used from 1979 to 1983 (*USER*) in each sector.[10] The majority of the innovations covered by the survey is used in sectors other than the sector of origin. The percentage clearly varies with the level of aggregation of the sector. Pavitt (1984) estimated that 75 per cent of the innovations at the three-digit level and 70 per cent at the two-digit level are used outside their sector of origin. The results of the rankings are given in Table 5.7, with 1 the highest and 22 the lowest (19 in the case of patents). The sectors are ranked according to the number of innovations produced in each sector; the last column shows the ratio between innovations produced and used. One of the main drawbacks in

Table 5.7 Ranking of technology variables

Industry	PROD	R&D	PAT	USER	PROD/USE
Machinery	1	8	1	1	2.24
Instruments	2	10	4	4	3.23
Electrical	3	7	6	3	2.14
Computers	4	5	13	10	2.33
Electronics	5	1	3	17	2.27
Chemicals	6	4	2	14	4.00
Other transport	7	22	10	7	1.28
Motor vehicles	8	6	8	5	0.76
Ships	9	20	19	17	4.00
Aerospace	9	2	9	7	0.85
Fabricated metals	11	13	5	13	1.22
Rubber and plastic	11	16	7	14	1.83
Textiles	13	17	14	2	0.26
Food	13	9	18	7	0.71
Paper	15	18	–	6	0.52
Glass	15	14	12	19	9.00
Wood	17	21	–	18	3.00
Pharmaceuticals	17	3	11	19	5.00
Other manufacturing	19	15	–	19	4.00
Oil refineries	19	11	17	16	0.60
Ferrous metals	21	12	15	12	0.30
Non-ferrous metals	22	19	16	22	2.00

using R&D expenditure data as a proxy for innovation is that it underestimates the contribution of small firms, which may not have the internal capacity to set up a separate research department and budget, but do nevertheless engage in innovatory activity. Direct counts of innovations, such as those taken from the SPRU survey, are better at reflecting the innovation activity of small firms, and are thus likely to be higher on a sector basis than R&D indicators in sectors characterized by small firms (Pavitt et al., 1987). Results using these data presented in Chapter 4 show that patents are closely correlated with innovations produced rather than either innovations used or R&D expenditure. There was no significant relationship between R&D expenditure and patents for this sample.

As can be seen from the table there is a large amount of variation between the technology variables. We would particularly expect a divergence between the output of patents and the input of R&D expenditure for those industries for which the results altered greatly with the change of technology variable. First, take those sectors with positively significant results using the patent variable but not with R&D, namely computers, electronics and instruments. The computer sector has a much higher position with respect to R&D than for patents, while electronics with the highest R&D expenditure is third in the ranking for patents. Both these sectors are high net producers of innovations, and spend more on R&D than they produce patents, relative to the other sectors. This indicates that the sectors are characterized by a fast pace of innovation, and that producers are possibly concerned over secrecy, and appropriating the benefits of innovation. For instruments, the ranking with patents is higher than with R&D and they are also net producers of innovations. Some sectors had positively significant results with R&D but not with patents. They all turn out to be net producers of innovations, with the exception of aerospace, and all have higher rankings in patents than R&D expenditure. Many innovations produced in these sectors may benefit sectors other than the sector of origin, so that not all have an advantageous effect on competitiveness in the sector of origin. The most important feature shown by Table 5.7 is the divergence between the different proxies of innovation; the rankings clearly show that different aspects of innovation are reflected by R&D expenditure, patents and counts of innovation. Thus using only one proxy may misrepresent the role of technology.

5.4.3 Innovation Counts and UK Trade Performance

In order to further investigate the relationship between innovation and bilateral trade these innovation variables are used as explanatory variables for the relationship already considered. As the innovation variables are only available for the UK, only the UK's bilateral trade flows with the other eight countries in the sample were used, making the number of observations 176. First, the earlier model was considered only for UK trade flows using the same specification with the log of bilateral trade as the dependent variable;

these are presented in the first two lines of Table 5.8. For the model using R&D expenditure the coefficients for the investment and R&D variables are positive but not significant using the *t*-test and labour is negatively significant.[11] With the RTA index in place of R&D intensity, the coefficient for the labour variable is still negative and the RTA variable itself is positive but not significant; the investment variable is negative but not significant. This is a problem of collinearity: the labour and investment variables are negatively correlated; a simple correlation between bilateral trade and investment is positive and significant. These results imply that innovation may not have a significantly positive impact on UK trade flows, which appear to be strongly influenced by relative labour costs.

As the innovation variables are absolute and reflect only the innovation pattern of the UK, not that of its partner countries, a net export variable, such as bilateral trade, may not be the most appropriate dependent variable for models including the innovation variables. As a result a different dependent variable is used, which gives gross rather than net exports. The variable is the log of UK bilateral exports on a cumulative basis from 1979 to 1988 with the eight OECD partners used before, scaled by production in each industry. The innovation variables used are for the five-year period from 1979 to 1983, logged and scaled by output in each sector. The denominator is introduced in order to provide a measure of industry dimension[12] which should reduce heteroscedasticity. The equation estimated is given below (equation 5.3), where *X* is cumulative exports, *P* cumulative production and *I* one of the innovation variables, either the innovations used or the innovations produced. Both the investment and labour variables are included as before. This model is also repeating using the R&D and RTA variables with the gross export variable as the dependent variable for comparison.

$$
\ln \left(\frac{X_{ukqs}}{P_{uks}} \right) = \alpha + \beta_1 \ln \left(\frac{W_{uks}}{W_{qs}} \right) + \beta_2 \ln \left(\frac{K_{uks}}{K_{qs}} \right)
$$
$$
+ \beta_3 \ln \left(\frac{I_{uks}}{P_{uks}} \right) + \varepsilon
$$

$$(5.3)$$

As can be seen from Table 5.8 the results change considerably using gross instead of net trade. There are some interesting points in the results. First the investment variable is negative using both the innovation variables (*PROD* and *USER*) and the RTA index rather than R&D expenditure, although it is significant in only one case. Second, the labour variable is positively and significantly related to gross exports, despite being negatively and significantly related to net exports in the earlier results. This gives some

Table 5.8 Results for the UK

I	α	W	K	I	R^2
Net exports					
R&D	−0.58***	−0.22***	0.24	0.12	0.11
	(0.22)	(0.06)	(0.21)	(0.11)	
RTA	−0.61***	−0.22***	−0.07	0.14	0.11
	(0.21)	(0.06)	(0.20)	(0.19)	
Gross exports					
R&D	0.57***	0.004*	0.0004	0.01**	0.08
	(0.01)	(0.002)	(0.008)	(0.004)	
RTA	0.57***	0.01***	−0.006	0.002	0.08
	(0.01)	(0.002)	(0.008)	(0.007)	
PROD	0.57***	0.01***	−0.01**	0.01***	0.14
	(0.01)	(0.002)	(0.007)	(0.003)	
USER	0.57***	0.01***	−0.01	0.01***	0.16
	(0.01)	(0.002)	(0.01)	(0.003)	

Notes:
*** Significant at 1%, ** at 5%, * at 10%.

evidence for the UK having high exports in areas with high labour costs, and hence we can assume higher skills. As the net trade balance is negatively affected by labour costs, the UK clearly has high imports in high-wage sectors as well as higher exports; it could be that intra-industry trade is larger in more-skilled sectors. There has been much discussion of the appropriate trade variable, particularly in the literature focusing on intra-industry trade. The export variable used here gives no estimate of the degree of intra-industry or inter-industry trade. This difference may be one of the explanations for the varying results on the labour coefficient.

Both of the innovation variables – innovations used and produced – are positively and significantly related to gross exports. The use of an innovation variable has a slightly better explanatory power than the production of innovations, although both explain more of gross exports than either of the two innovation proxies. Thus when considering gross, rather than net UK trade, there appears to be a positive relationship between innovation and the UK's trade performance. As the innovation variables used in this subsection are only available for the UK, a relative innovation variable could not be used, and gross exports scaled by production is more appropriate. The results indicate that both the use and production of innovations has a positive impact on exports.

To summarize, UK gross exports are positively influenced by innovations – both used and produced – and by labour costs; higher labour costs are positively related to higher exports, indicating a competitive advantage in skilled labour sectors. Investment, on the other hand, is negatively related to exports. The next section investigates the relationship between the production and use of innovation in some more detail. As the innovation variables are only available from this survey for the UK, alternative methods are used in the next section to investigate the impact of innovation on trade for the whole sample of OECD countries.

5.5 PRODUCERS AND USERS OF INNOVATIONS AND TRADE PERFORMANCE

From the sector-level results it is clear that there is a great deal of variation in the relationship between innovation and export performance over sectors. In this last section an attempt is made to consider the sectors divided into two groups based on their innovation characteristics. Pavitt (1984) has made a taxonomy of sectors, based on the innovation data from the SPRU data base also used in this chapter. He described a three-fold taxonomy based on: the sources of innovations used by the sector; the sources and nature of the innovations produced; and the characteristics of the innovating firms. Here a much simpler classification is used (see Amable and Verspagen, 1995, for one application of the Pavitt taxonomy to estimates of trade performance). In this section, sectors are classified either as net users or as net producers of innovations. As Robson et al. (1988) have pointed out, five core sectors (chemicals, machinery, mechanical engineering, instruments and electronics) account for 64 per cent of all innovations included in the survey. They also note two important trends in the production and use of technology. The first is that sectors are becoming increasingly technologically interdependent, with process innovations (defined as innovations produced and used within the same sector) declining as a proportion of total innovations. The second is that an increasing proportion of product innovations are being used outside manufacturing sectors. One example is the application of electronics to service sectors such as banking and retail.

The majority of innovation spillovers comes from a limited number of sectors, which provide innovations used not just in firms in the same sector, but also in firms located in different sectors. We would expect R&D expenditure to be important in influencing the trade performance of these producer industries. However, as other work on the survey has pointed out some of the high producers of innovations undertake very little formal R&D expenditure, but rather the innovations occur because of the nature of the dominant technology used in the sector. For instance, small specialized firms in the mechanical engineering sector produce many product innovations which pass to other sectors, while having no internal R&D expenditure. Nevertheless, despite this heterogeneity, we would expect innovation-producing sectors to have their trade performance strongly influenced by innovation, proxied by R&D expenditure.

The innovation survey is used in this section to separate sectors into users and producers of innovations. In order to do so, the last column of Table 5.7 was consulted and those sectors which have a production to use of innovation ratio higher than one were taken as being producers of innovations while those with a ratio of less than one were assumed to be users of innovations.[13] The assumption is made that the sectoral ratio of production to use of innovations for the UK can be applied to the same sectors in other countries of the sample; this generalization is necessary as the ratio is only available for the UK. In addition, there are some sectors which have ratios very close to one, which appear to be neither net users nor net producers of innovations, but instead use and produce a similar number of innovations. For those sectors (such as fabricated metals and aerospace), the categorization into either a user or a producer of technology is arbitrary. As a result, the model was re-estimated taking producers as those with a ratio over 1.2 and users with a ratio below 0.8; this change in classification made a negligible difference to the results, and the results are not presented here. As the ratios show little change between the entire period of the survey (1945 to 1983) and the last five years of the survey, the choice is not important and the latter are used in the calculations.

The data for the OECD sample of countries were then pooled into two different groups – producers and users of innovations. This separation was tested against the restricted model with the producers and users of technology being pooled together. The innovation variable used was R&D expenditure in order to include the greatest number of industries. The unrestricted model is given below where X is a vector of explanatory variables. The empirical model tested is:

$$\frac{X_{pqs}}{X_{qps}} = \alpha + \beta_1 X_i + \beta_2 X_i + \varepsilon \qquad (5.4)$$

where: $\beta_1 = 1$ when i is a producer industry and 0 elsewhere, $\beta_2 = 1$ when i is a user industry and 0 elsewhere, and X_i is a matrix of explanatory variables. The restriction on the explanatory variables was rejected at 1 per cent using a heteroscedastic consistent F-test, while the restriction on the intercept was not rejected. As a result, the model here was with a single intercept and separate explanatory variables for the two groups. The separation was also repeated for the subsample of UK trade flows to check the consistency of the results for the subsample. The pooling restriction was rejected for the UK subsample at 1 per cent. The results are given in Table 5.9 for both the whole sample and for the UK.

Table 5.9 Producers and users of innovations

	Investment	Labour	R&D
Producers–OECD	0.89	−0.18	0.45
	(0.15)***	(0.04)***	(0.11)***
Users–OECD	0.67	−0.11	0.05
	(0.21)***	(0.04)***	(0.08)
Producers–UK	0.46	−0.23	0.43
	(0.23)**	(0.07)***	(0.15)***
Users–UK	−0.03	−0.21	−0.16
	(0.37)	(0.08)***	(0.15)

Notes:
OECD sample: $\alpha = -0.10$ (0.07), $R^2 = 0.13$. UK: $\alpha = -0.59$ (0.22)***, $R^2 = 0.17$.
** Significant at 5%, *** at 1%.

For the OECD countries investment is positively and significantly related to trade performance; and labour costs are negatively and significantly related for both net users and producers of innovations. The main difference is in the R&D variable where the coefficient is positive for both producers and users of technology; it is significant only for the producers of technology. This indicates that R&D expenditure is 'rational' for net producers of technology as they are successfully improving their trade performance, although this is not the case for net users of technology for whom R&D expenditure appears to have little impact on trade performance. In the case of the users of innovation, it is likely to be the diffusion of innovation which has the greatest impact on trade performance.

The UK results also show variations across producers and users of innovations. Both investment and R&D expenditure are negatively (but not significantly) related to trade performance for the users in the UK sample, but positive and significant for the producers of innovations. Both R&D and investment appear to have a much greater positive impact on trade performance for the producers of innovations than for the users. It is consistent that the producers of technology would also find investment more important in influencing trade performance as innovating may require higher levels of investment than the use of innovations.

To summarize, many of the innovations in the survey are used by firms other than the firm of origin, and often in a different sector from the sector of origin. In these user sectors, R&D expenditure appears to have a limited impact on trade performance. However, R&D expenditure does have a positive role in trade performance for the innovating sectors.

5.6 CONCLUSIONS

The objective of this chapter was to examine the empirical determinants of bilateral trade between nine OECD countries, and in particular to assess the impact of differences in innovation on trade performance. The results point to the importance of innovation in influencing bilateral trade performance. Considering the results that are consistent with our *a priori* expectations and using either of the two proxies, 15 out of the 22 sectors in the sectoral model showed a positive and significant relationship between relative innovation and bilateral trade performance. For the labour-cost variable, eleven sectors showed negatively significant results using one or other proxy, and three positively significant results. This gives very little evidence for the skills hypothesis even on a sectoral level, although for two of the three sectors – computers and pharmaceuticals – the skills hypothesis is credible. For the relative investment variable, eleven sectors had positively significant results; the results were much better using the patent proxy than with the R&D proxy, because of collinearity between investment and R&D expenditure. Overall, the innovation variable is a significant factor in a larger number of sectors than either relative investment or relative labour costs, indicating an important role for differences in innovation in explaining bilateral trade performance. For a number of sectors it is clearly a combination of factors which is important, and no single factor explains bilateral trade performance.

The relationship appears to vary considerably over both sectors and countries. Important country effects exist, reflecting the importance of country-specific features such as economic structure, institutions, the exchange rate and trade relations which affect bilateral trade in all sectors. The relationship between the explanatory variables and trade performance, on the other hand, varies considerably over sectors, that is, the significance of relative labour costs, investment and innovation, depend on the sector being considered. Thus for sectors such as pharmaceuticals, innovation is clearly a key factor affecting trade performance regardless of which pair of countries is taken. Many of the medium-technology manufacturing sectors such as fabricated metals and rubber and plastic appear to be influenced both by low labour costs and relative R&D expenditure, again regardless of the countries being considered.

Actual innovations are also used as an indication of innovation at the sectoral level for the UK; they are divided into innovations used and innovations produced in each sector. Both innovations used and produced were found to have a positive effect on gross exports for the UK, indicating that both innovation itself and the diffusion of innovation to other sectors within the country, have a positive impact on trade performance. Actual innovation counts were also used to separate sectors into innovators and users of innovations, and to see if this difference altered the relationship between the explanatory factors and trade performance. It was found that the R&D variable has more impact on trade performance for the innovators than the users of innovations. Therefore, attempts to group sectors together based on common characteristics should perhaps consider whether the sector is a net user or net producer of innovations. This characteristic appears to affect the impact of R&D expenditure on trade performance, which also has important implications for both technology and industrial policy. For a country which is attempting to improve its competitiveness via, for instance, subsidies to R&D expenditure, the effectiveness of such a policy will depend in a large part on the structure of the domestic economy. Subsidies given to sectors which are net producers of innovations are likely to have a larger positive impact on export performance than those given to the net users of innovations. In addition, as both the use and the production of innovations appear to have a positive impact on exports (see the results for the UK), the innovations coming from the innovation-producing sectors have a beneficial effect not just on exports in those sectors but also on sectors which subsequently use the innovations. As other observers have pointed out (Dalum, 1992), the core innovating sectors are of great importance to the economy in general, as they generate a large number of innovations of benefit to the whole economy.

The existence of differences in innovation between the countries of the sample, and their role in explaining variations in bilateral trade performance, also have implications for the economic convergence of countries. The national systems of innovation of different countries lead to the specialization of some countries in sectors in which there is a rapid rate of technical change, and in which high rates of innovation are required, which has implications for the growth pattern of countries. The analysis presented here is a static one, examining the role of differences in innovation on trade in the 1980s. However, dynamic analyses also point to the continuing importance of differences in innovation on long-run trade performance, and it is clear that innovation is a key feature in competitiveness with important implications for trade in a wide selection of sectors. Differences in innovation remain even between industrialized countries such as those considered here, so technology cannot be characterized as a public good which is immediately diffused between countries. Rather, information is costly and can be partly appropriated by the innovator. As a result, innovation can remain country and sector specific and provide a competitive advantage to countries, and sectors within countries.

NOTES

1. See Fagerberg (1994b) for an overview of the relationship between technology and international differences in growth rates.
2. Soete and Verspagen (1992) test a model of dynamic technology gaps and their impact on convergence.
3. For a dynamic model of the impact of differences of innovation on long-run trade performance using the same data, see Verspagen and Wakelin (1997a).
4. The RTA index is analogous to comparative advantage. The data for patents are not available for three of the industries, they are: wood, cork and furniture; paper and printing; and other manufacturing industries. The home bias of the US is taken account of in the index, as the index is relative rather than absolute, and thus is not influenced by the absolute number of patents – which is higher for the US than other countries – but rather their sectoral distribution.
5. The number of missing variables depends on the variables included. The sample always has more than 500 observations.
6. There is some collinearity between the investment variable and R&D expenditure, explaining the variation in the coefficient on investment.
7. Industry 22 (other transport) was omitted because of inadequate data.
8. It should be noted that each country model does not have the same number of bilateral flows. The model for Canada has all eight and each of the following countries has one less with Sweden having only one bilateral relationship with the US which is not included separately. This gives incomplete results for each country and added importance to the result for Canada in which R&D expenditure is positive and significant.
9. A relative patent intensity index which is analogous to relative R&D intensity was also used. However, it was collinear with the investment variable and as a result was dropped from the calculations.
10. Using the innovations for the entire period 1945 to 1983 instead of for the five-year period does not change the ranking of the sectors.

11. These results differ from those in Table 5.2 because of the inclusion of all the UK's bilateral trade flows, including those with Canada, Germany and France which were previously included with the partner countries.
12. See Deardorff (1984). The introduction of the denominator does not affect the significance of the results.
13. Scherer (1982) testing the relationship between demand–pull and technological opportunity in influencing innovation, considers sectors as users or producers of innovations based on patent data.

APPENDIX 5A THE SECTORAL BREAKDOWN, SOURCES AND SIC CODES

The sectoral breakdown that is used corresponds to ISIC, revision 2. The ISIC-codes per sector are given below in the first column, followed by the name of the sector and then the SIC 1968 codes given after the name.

Table 5A.1 SIC codes

ISIC code	name	SIC code
3100	food	2100–2400
3200	textiles	4100–4400 (excluding 4291)
3300	wood	4710–4793
3400	paper and publishing	4810–1890
3510+3520–3522	chemicals	2700–2797 (excluding 2720)
3522	pharmaceuticals	2720
3530+3540	refined oil	2610–2630
3560+3570	rubber and plastic products	4910–4960
3600	glass etc.	4620–4691
3710	ferrous metals	3110–3130
3720	nonferrous metals	3210–3230
3810	fabricated metal	3910–3999
3820–3825	machinery	3300–3493
3825	computers	3660+3661
3830–3832:	electrical	3600–3620, 3670–3695
3832	electronics	3630–3652
3841	ships	3700–3702
3843	motor vehicles	3810
3845	aerospace	3830–3834
3840–3841–3843–3845	other transport	3800+3820+3840+3850
3850	instruments	3510–3542
3900	other manufacturing	4920–4950+4990–4992

Data on bilateral exports were used to calculate the trade balance variables. These data were supplied by the OECD in the ISIC classification (taken from the bilateral trade database). Because these data are originally available in the SITC classification, the OECD Secretariat has used a self-developed correspondence table to supply data in ISIC. Data on R&D were also supplied by the OECD. R&D is undertaken by business enterprises, but might be financed by any source. Missing values in this data set were filled by analytical methods (the so-called ANBERD database). The data on military and government-financed R&D are taken from the Basic Science and Technology database of the OECD. Data on the wage rate were calculated by using the total wage costs, the number of employees and the current exchange rate. All variables came from the STAN database of the OECD.

PART III

Technology and the International Economic
Performance of Firms

6. Innovation and Exports at the Firm Level

This chapter aims to analyse the role of firm-specific competitive advantages in determining the export behaviour of firms. In order to do so two groups of firms are examined: innovating and non-innovating firms. A combination of microeconomic and macroeconomic determinants of exports are considered, encompassing both firm-specific characteristics and the characteristics of the sector in which the firm is operating; particular emphasis is given to the innovation characteristics of both the firm and the sector. The main focus is on the interaction between a firm's innovation capabilities, the technological opportunity at the sector level and firm export behaviour.

The chapter can be divided into two parts. Sections 1 and 2 provide background to the model estimated later in the chapter; Sections 3 to 5 give an outline of the data set used, and present the empirical model and results. In the first half, Section 1 links the concept of firm competitiveness used in this chapter, to the macroeconomic concept of competitiveness upon which the rest of the study is based. It also gives an outline of other empirical work concerning the determinants of exports at the firm level. Section 2 gives a brief overview of recent UK trade performance, as the firms considered in this chapter are all UK firms.

In the second half of the chapter, Section 3 presents the empirical model to be tested and discusses our *a priori* expectations of the results. Section 4 outlines the data set used, with information on the selection of both the innovating and non-innovating firms. It also gives some descriptive statistics which highlight differences between the two groups of firms. Section 5 describes the method of estimation, and gives the results for the probability of a firm exporting, and for the propensity of firms to export. The model is then re-estimated for the quoted firms alone, in Section 6, as firm-level R&D expenditure are available for those firms. The results show the importance of firm-specific characteristics in determining firm-level exports, in particular for the innovating firms. The sector-specific characteristics – domestic market size and sector innovation levels – appear to be more important for the non-innovating firms than the innovating firms. Overall, this microeconomic analysis confirms the importance of innovation in determining exports. Finally, Section 7 gives some conclusions and the policy implications of the analysis.

6.1 FIRM COMPETITIVENESS

The earlier chapters have concentrated on the impact of differences in innovation on trade performance at the sector and country level. As the central focus of this study is innovation, and the impact on trade performance of differences in technological capabilities, a logical extension of this work is to consider the relationship between innovation and export performance at the firm level. It is at the level of the firm that technological accumulation occurs; firms can create a specific competitive advantage through innovation because of the cumulative nature of innovation and innovatory capabilities (Kay, 1982; Dosi and Chiaromonte, 1990). It is at the firm level that decisions about the commitment of resources to innovation and the innovative strategy of the firm are made. It is also principally at the level of the firm that the benefits of innovation are enjoyed, in terms of cost reductions in the case of process innovations, and new markets and potential monopoly rents in the case of product innovations. The sector, and more broadly the country, in which the firm is located provides the context for these decisions, and both clearly have a strong influence on them.

6.1.1 Innovation Within the Firm

Nelson and Winter (1982), place firms at the centre of their analysis of technical change as an evolutionary process. The analysis is highly detailed, but some of the most relevant points concerning firm behaviour, and the environment in which firms are located, are summarized below.

1. The environment the firms are located in is not in equilibrium; instead it is in a constant state of change and is characterized by uncertainty. Technological change is a dynamic force repeatedly changing the environment and destroying equilibria, and this acts as a dynamic selection mechanism for firms.
2. Firms within this environment are not maximizing profits, but rather exhibiting satisficing behaviour and are not aware of an infinite set of possibilities. As a result, firms are heterogeneous, and may vary

considerably in terms of production methods, efficiency and their approach to innovation.

3. The search for new decision rules to follow is *local*, that is, firms are constrained by their present attributes and knowledge which limits their potential for change, as well as being limited by the industry in which they are located, in their search for new techniques. This leads to path dependency in terms of the growth of the firm, and in particular for the innovative activities of the firm, with past activities influencing future decisions. Through the process of innovation some firms become more competitive relative to others, providing an incentive for others firms to follow the innovator; this leads to technical progress at the level of the sector and the economy over time.

Together these, and a number of other assumptions referring to the market and firms, have been used by Nelson and Winter (1974, 1982) and others (Dosi, 1988; Dosi et al., 1988) to create an evolutionary approach to economic growth.

Within this evolutionary tradition innovation is considered to be of central importance. Certain features of innovation highlighted by (among others) Dosi (1984, 1988) and Freeman (1982), lead to the accumulation of innovation at the level of the firm. This means that one innovation makes another related innovation more likely, so that firms become specialized in particular technological areas. Among the features of innovation which are important are: the tacit and non-codifiable nature of technology; the importance of learning by doing and learning by using in technological change; and the potential to appropriate some of the benefits of innovation. As technology is not always codifiable, the transfer and diffusion of it can occur only slowly, combined with learning via the production process and the implementation of new innovations; firms accumulate skills and knowledge. Innovation becomes a cumulative process (Rosenberg, 1976, 1982) which is specific to the firm. Technology is thus embodied both in people and in firms (Teece, 1986).

The level of uncertainty associated with innovation leads to the second point, that firms do not necessarily maximize their profits. Instead, firms can be characterized as 'boundedly rational' (Simon, 1986). Firms are thus *profit seeking* and base this search on their current knowledge and capabilities, which reflects their immediate environment. Because of the general level of uncertainty, and in particular uncertainty in relation to innovation, firms are unaware of all the alternatives that are available to them (Freeman, 1982); they search for new innovations locally which, combined with the cumulative nature of innovation, leads to the importance of past experience. As Dosi

(1988, p. 1130) put it: 'what a firm can hope to do technologically in the future is narrowly constrained by what it has been capable of doing in the past'. The result is that technological change at the level of the firm is *path dependent* with past experience affecting present innovation potential. One outcome from these firm-specific innovation patterns is that asymmetries exist between firms in terms of their technological capabilities and their general economic performance, including their trade performance. Firms have differentiated learning patterns which alter their ability to perceive and exploit innovation opportunities (Silverberg et al., 1988); the benefits of innovation are at least partly appropriable, and as a result innovation gives an ownership advantage to the firm.

The importance of the firm in the process of innovation was implicitly acknowledged by the early theories relating innovation to trade performance. Posner (1961), in his technology gap model of trade, considered that the temporary advantage in knowledge which gave rise to a trade advantage was industry specific. Nevertheless, Posner considered dynamic economies of scale, resulting from learning, as occurring at the level of the firm, and being firm specific. Firms in particular countries produce innovations, which other domestic firms in the industry are assumed to be able to react to faster than firms abroad; foreign firms experience a learning lag. As a result, the benefit of the innovation is felt by the domestic sector of the innovating firm, before the same sector in foreign countries. Thus the benefits of innovation are felt not just by the innovating firm, but by the whole domestic industry. Posner also provides an outline of which factors may lead to a single innovation becoming a stream of innovations over time. These factors include: that innovations come in clusters because of technical connections between them; that analogously demand-side complementarities lead to further pressure for innovations in related products; and that each sector's commitment to research and investment varies. So the forces which act to give innovating sectors a long-term innovation advantage, can also act at the firm level, to give the firm an innovative advantage over time.

Firms' innovation patterns are also constrained by the nature of the technology they deal with, and the technological characteristics of the sectors in which they operate. Different technological paradigms (Dosi, 1984) have different characteristics; for instance, some may be more reliant on basic scientific research, others on cumulative experience, and these alter the characteristics of the firms involved with the technology (Pavitt, 1984). At the sector level, the limitations of science, and of the specific technology, act as one constraint on firms (some things just cannot be invented), and each technology is also characterized by the economic opportunities which it presents. Together both of these factors vary with the sector in which the firm is located, and the technology upon which it is based. Some sectors, such as mechanical engineering, have a high level of technical opportunity as a result of the production process, while others, such as footwear and clothing, offer a much lower level of technological opportunity. The probability of a firm being an innovator is much higher in some sectors because of the higher level of technological opportunity in those sectors. There are also other industry-specific benefits as well as technological opportunity which influence firms, such as the demand conditions in the sector. Aharoni and Hirsch (1993) divide products into those which contain an important element of firm-specific proprietary knowledge (S-products), and those which do not depend on such knowledge and are based on universally available knowledge (U-products). It is the former that are most influenced by firm-specific competitive advantage, and the latter by the relative costs of inputs other than knowledge.

Firm competitiveness, as well as being influenced by firm-specific characteristics, such as management skills and innovation, is also influenced by the more general economic structure in which the firm is located. The 'structural competitiveness' (Chesnais, 1986) of the country also affects firm competitiveness. As Chesnais (1992, p. 267) put it: 'their competitiveness will also stem from economy-specific long term trends in the strength and efficiency of a national economy's productive structure, its technical infra-structure and other factors determining the externalities on which firms can build'.

A number of different factors can affect a country's structural competitiveness, including the size of the domestic market, the structure of domestic relations between different sectors and the size distribution of firms. As Chesnais (1992) points out, the increasing importance of generic technologies, such as microelectronics, means that the interrelations between different sectors in terms of transfers of technology is of increasing importance to the structure of the economy. Together these technological characteristics make up the national system of innovation of that country. It should be noted that the national system of innovation of a particular country is more than the sum of the innovation experiences of its firms; country-level factors such as institutions and government policy, as well as the interactions between firms and sectors, add an additional dimension to the national system of innovation. There have been a number of studies recently considering national systems of innovation, and the impact they have on a country's pattern and speed of development.[1] The *localized* nature of search for innovations, discussed earlier in the context of firms, also applies at the national level, and is one reason why, even with global production and integrated economies, it is possible to talk of *national* patterns of innovation. The importance of institutions and the cumulative nature of innovation emphasize that a country's history and culture shape its subsequent innovation profile, that is, technological development is path dependent at the macroeconomic as well as at the microeconomic level (David, 1975; Arthur, 1989).

6.1.2 International Firm Performance

The connection between firm-specific innovation advantages, which give the firm a competitive advantage relative to other firms, and a country's comparative advantage has received very little attention. One argument that has been put forward is that the position of a sector within a country can be influenced by comparative advantage, but firm-specific characteristics may not conform to a country's comparative advantage. Within a sector in which a country has a comparative disadvantage, some firms may still have a competitive advantage relative to foreign competitors, and likewise in sectors which have a comparative advantage, some firms may be in a weak position relative to foreign competitors. This argument has been presented by Abd-el-Rahman (1991) as one explanation for intra-industry trade. He states that trade is explained both by a country's pattern of comparative advantage, but also by the individual performances of firms within each sector. As he points out, the inclusion of a microeconomic perspective on trade is only possible if the assumptions of perfect competition are discarded, in order to allow heterogeneity between firms. Variations in the capabilities of firms will lead to variations in firm performance, including firms' ability to export. Abd-el-Rahman frames this variation in firm performance within the structure of comparative advantage which influences the development of sectors within a country. Within each sector there is a spectrum of firm behaviour and firms can be ranked according to their general performance. While major export patterns can be explained by comparative advantage, there will also be minor trade flows which are contrary to comparative advantage and are explained by firm-specific advantages.

Hirsch and Bijaoui (1985) argue that firms' competitive advantages can be independent of factor intensities, but at the same time there is not necessarily a contradiction between the Heckscher–Ohlin approach to trade and firm advantages. The latter may be consistent with factor endowments, making more intensive use of the more abundant factors of production. Alternatively, competitive advantage may be based on the superior proprietary knowledge of a firm in a way unrelated to factor intensities. They consider export performance at the firm level as they judge the firm to be 'the organization which translates the abstract notion of comparative advantage into reality by designing, producing and marketing goods and services' (p. 240).

The competitive advantage of firms is an absolute advantage over other firms. Comparative advantage acts at the level of the country and influences the pattern of trade specialization of a country, and thus the sectoral structure. The competitive advantage of firms may be compatible, and interact with, comparative advantage, as in the Abd-el-Rahman approach, or to contradict it. In the work of Dosi et al. (1990) already discussed, absolute differences in technology are considered to be more important than endowment-based comparative advantage in explaining trade patterns. In their framework, within the trade pattern set out by absolute differences in technology, comparative cost considerations may be relevant, but it is absolute differences in technology which predominate. The interaction of firm-based competitive advantages, and a country's specialization pattern have traditionally been treated as separate, the former being considered as an international business issue, and the latter being left to international trade economists. The neo-classical basis of much of international trade theory has explicitly ruled out the role of the firm, because of the assumption of perfect competition. With multinational companies (MNCs) dominating trade, the assumption of equally–sized atomistic firms and constant returns to scale are becoming increasingly hard to hang on to, and the importance of firm-specific characteristics needs also to be included in approaches to international trade.

It is in the context of foreign direct investment (FDI) by MNCs that firm-specific competitive advantages have been most widely considered.[2] Such advantages provide one motivation for the internalization of a firm's activities, which occurs when creating an MNC. The 'eclectic theory' of Dunning (1981, 1993) considers the interaction between firm-specific advantages, in particular monopoly advantages, and the benefits to be gained from internalization, and the advantages of the point of location of the MNC. Firm-specific advantages interact with location advantages to explain a firm's preference for direct production overseas rather than servicing the foreign market through exports, or licensing, or other forms of arm's-length transactions. But the same firm-specific advantages also give a firm a competitive advantage on *export* markets. As in the technology gap model, unique innovations give the innovator monopoly power, for as long as the innovation is not diffused abroad, it can have a positive impact on the firm's export performance. If that temporary monopoly advantage is supplemented by dynamic economies of scale, then a single firm may have a long-term technological superiority on export markets. Seen in this way, the technology gap theory refers to firms (and in Posner's argument by extension the domestic industry), which embody the technological advantage; as a result it seems appropriate to add a microeconomic empirical analysis to the sector-level and country-level analyses of the earlier chapters.

6.1.3 Firm Innovation and Export Behaviour

This final empirical chapter aims to address the importance of firm-specific competitive advantage on exports, by considering the impact of innovation on export performance at the microeconomic level, using firm data for 500 UK firms. The emphasis will be on the competitive advantage of firms, rather than on the comparative advantage of the UK. The relative strengths and weaknesses of the UK economy, that is, its comparative advantage, are not addressed; instead the innovation characteristics, both of the firm and of the sector of the firm, are assessed as determinants of firm-level export performance. In contrast to other microeconomic studies, which have taken R&D expenditure as an indicator of innovation, this chapter uses the innovation history of the firms to categorize them into innovators and non-innovators.

Innovation is considered as a characteristic which fundamentally changes the firm and its performance, including the firm's export performance. This view of technology implies that the process of innovation differentiates innovating firms from non-innovating firms; thus innovation is not just a random process which occurs for some firms and not for others. As a result we would expect to see a difference in the relationship between the determinants of trade and export performance for the two groups of firms – innovators and non-innovators. The question is not whether a specific innovation helps to increase the market position of a firm in the short run by, for instance, conferring above-normal profits due to a temporary monopoly which subsequently improves export performance. Rather, it is whether the process of innovation increases a firm's capabilities which in turn has a permanent effect on the performance of that firm. The hypothesis of differences between innovators and non-innovating firms is tested in the context of export performance, to see if the determinants of exports for the two groups of firms in the sample, the innovating firms and the non-innovating firms, can be estimated with the two groups together or if they should be separated.

Another issue which this chapter wishes to address is the impact of innovation on export performance. The interaction of sector-level innovation and firm–specific innovation on exports is also considered, that is, an attempt is made to separate the effects of being in an innovative sector from the firm-specific effects of in-house innovation on exports. To this end, both sector-level and firm-level innovation variables are used. These two issues are clearly related: if innovating and non-innovating firms behave differently, then separate models need to be estimated for each group, and the relative importance of firm and sector technology factors on trade should be considered separately for the two groups.

Considering the relationship between innovation and exports for firms in a single country also has its own limitations. The exports of each firm give no indication of the imported content of the firm's output, or of the level of import penetration within the industry in which the firm operates. Thus each firm's exports are not considered within the wider context of the country's pattern of trade performance, but rather relative to the characteristics of that firm and the structure of the sector in which it is located. Innovation variables, both for the sector and for the firm, show domestic technological capabilities, but do not give those capabilities relative to sectors and firms in other countries. Instead, the framework examines the domestic firm-level and sector-level determinants of export performance, and not those characteristics relative to foreign competitors. In this sense the analysis is radically different from that already presented at the macroeconomic level, which took differences in innovation across countries and within sectors as one of the main determinants of trade performance. The next subsection considers some empirical work carried out at the firm level.

6.1.4 Evidence at the Firm Level

Most firm-level studies considering innovation have concentrated on testing the Schumpeterian hypothesis of a positive relationship between firm size and innovation. However, a number of studies have examined the relationship between innovation and exports. Kumar and Siddharthan (1994) analysed the relationship between R&D expenditure and exports for 640 Indian firms from 1988 to 1990, grouped according to industry. They found R&D expenditure to be an important factor in low-technology and medium-technology industries, and they concluded that India does not have a competitive advantage in high-technology sectors, but innovation positively influences its performance in other sectors. Willmore (1992) concentrated on the role of transnationals in Brazil's trade, estimating both the determinants of exports and those of imports. He found no significant role for R&D expenditure as a determinant of exports, although R&D appeared to play a small negative role with respect to imports, indicating that technological effort led to increased domestic inputs and less reliance on imports. Both these studies used firm-level R&D expenditure as an indication of innovation, and thus neglected those firms which innovate without undertaking R&D *per se*.

Hirsch and Bijaoui (1985) considered the relationship between R&D expenditure and export performance for a small country, Israel, which has also seen a rapid rise in its exports for the period considered (the 1970s). The work aimed to test the importance of innovation advantages for 111 Israeli firms, all of which had undertaken R&D expenditure and were thus classified as innovators. Initially, the authors contrasted the propensity to export of their innovating firms with the average propensity to export in each sector, and found that the innovating firms, grouped into sectors, had a higher propensity to export than the sector average. In the cross-section model which followed, with the rate of change in exports of 1979–81 relative to 1975–77 as the dependent variable, they found R&D expenditure in 1977 to be a significant explanatory variable, along with the change in firm sales, taken as an indicator of 'other firm characteristics'. The firm-size variable (the logarithm of sales in 1981) was not found to affect the rate of change in exports, having an elasticity of approximately one. Thus they concluded that innovation is an important factor in explaining export performance, and that while a minimum size is probably required to export, beyond that firm size is not a major factor.

Glejser et al. (1980) used an extensive microeconomic data set of Belgian exporting firms to analyse the relationship between domestic and foreign market structure and export performance. There were no non-exporting firms in the sample, which consisted of 1,446 exporting firms; the firms were aggregated into sectors for the purpose of the study. No additional information was available at the firm level, apart from sales and exports; with the exception of some survey responses which were used as dummy variables in the analysis, sales were used as an indicator of firm size. The authors found firm size, industrial concentration, product differentiation, lack of information, location and foreign subsidiaries to all be important determinants of export behaviour. No variables were included for innovation, as the emphasis of the paper was the relationship between market structure and firm performance. The authors concluded that market structure variables are important determinants of firm-level exports.

Most of the firm-level studies share the use of R&D expenditure as an indicator of innovation, and as a basis for the classification for firms as innovators. Using the actual number of innovations that firms have had, as in this chapter, has the benefit of not excluding those firms not large enough to have a separate R&D department, or even an R&D budget, yet nevertheless innovate. The distribution of such firms may be concentrated in some sectors, such as the engineering and instrumentation sectors, in which many innovations are produced as part of the production process rather than through R&D.[3] By using the actual number of innovations produced to classify firms as innovators, the size bias of R&D expenditure as an innovation proxy can be avoided.

There are a considerable number of firm-level studies looking at the relationship between innovation and firm size, a controversial issue in the economics of technical change since Schumpeter, and in addition the relationship between firm size and export performance.[4] Scherer (1965) concentrated on the 500 largest US firms to consider the relationship between market structure, firm size and invention. More recently Acs and Audretsch (1988) have considered actual data on US innovations, similar to those used in this study for the UK. They concluded that large and small firms have different determinants of their innovative output. Pavitt et al. (1987) considered the size distribution of innovations for the UK, using the SPRU innovation survey data also applied in this chapter. They found that the relationship varied from that observed using R&D expenditure in place of innovations, with firms with fewer than 1,000 employees having more innovations than indicated by R&D expenditure data. As far as exports are concerned, a positive relationship between exports and firm size is generally expected. Bonaccorsi (1992) gives an overview of the export-marketing literature, which hypothesizes a positive relationship between exports and firm size based on economies of scale, the limited managerial and financial resources of small firms, and the assessment of risk in foreign markets. Because of the complex relationship between innovation and firm size, it is necessary to take account of firm size when considering the relationship between export performance and innovation.

Following on the idea that firms which innovate are different from non-innovating firms, Geroski and Machin (1993) have considered the relationship between profits, sales growth and innovation at the firm level, utilizing innovation data also taken from the SPRU survey. They found that there were 'generic differences' between innovating and non-innovating firms, for which the determinants of sales and profits appeared to differ. The clearest difference they observed was that innovating firms are less affected by cyclical shocks than non-innovating firms, providing some evidence for differences between innovating and other firms in terms of the impact of the business cycle. Whether or not this difference can be seen between innovating and non-innovating firms in terms of their export performance will be the focus of this chapter.

6.2 UK TRADE PERFORMANCE

The importance of innovation in affecting trade performance is of particular interest in the case of the UK. As numerous observers and studies have pointed out, the UK's trade performance in manufacturing, as shown by the UK share in world manufacturing trade, has been declining for much of the post-war period, although this trend may have been reversed in the 1980s.

Landesmann and Snell (1989) find that with the recession of 1979–81, and the supply-side legislation of the Conservative government, the UK economy restructured towards higher value-added sectors, and the income elasticity of demand for UK exports rose as a result. Anderton (1992) analysed the long-term trend decline in UK manufacturing exports using stochastic trend procedures. He concluded that the underlying decline in the UK export market share has not been at a constant rate over time. Using a number of different profitability variables as proxies for non-price competitiveness, he found that the decline had been decelerating in the 1980s, although the results were sensitive to the profit proxy being used.

Whether or not the decline has slowed down, or even been reversed, has been questioned by other authors (for instance, Temple, 1994) who note the negative impact of the recession on the accumulation of capital and technology so vital in establishing competitiveness. It is frequently noted (see, for instance, Thirlwall, 1986) that it is in the area of non-price competitiveness that the UK economy is particularly weak; this reflects, among other factors, the poor skills of the workforce, poor product design and quality, after-sales service and reliability.[5]

There have been a number of studies investigating the impact of non-price competitiveness on UK trade. Greenhalgh (1990) highlights the importance of non-price factors, including both innovation and reliability (proxied by the number of strikes), in influencing the UK's trade performance. She concludes that innovation sustains trade performance subject to considerable sector variations. For about half of the sectors examined, innovations used and produced in those sectors benefited trade performance (the source of the innovation data is the SPRU database also used in this chapter), but a number of important innovation-producing sectors did not appear to have improved trade performance as a result of their innovations. Buxton et al. (1991), in a study of five industrialized countries including the UK, concluded that relative expenditure on R&D was an important determinant of trade performance between the countries, and that expenditure on R&D constitutes a vital strategic investment because of the cumulative benefits of increasing the stock of R&D capital.

Another theme in the discussion of UK competitiveness has been the role of poor skills and human capital in affecting the UK's trade performance with other industrialized countries. As far as the skills of the UK workforce are concerned, Oulton (1996) finds differences in skills to be an important determinant of the UK's poor trade performance with respect to Germany.[6] In an earlier study, Katrak (1982) concluded that in the decade prior to 1978 the skill and R&D intensity of UK imports was rising relative to UK exports, while the opposite occurred for capital intensity, indicating a declining comparative advantage in skilled labour. Temple (1994), in a study of the evolution of the UK's trading performance, concludes that there is a skill gap which affects trade performance, in particular in the engineering industries, and that the basic training of the workforce may be one of the most important areas of weakness for the UK economy.

The trading experience of the UK in part reflects its national system of innovation, with its traditional strengths in the defence industries and pharmaceuticals, and low civil expenditure on research and development (Walker, 1993). In particular, the importance of military expenditure on R&D, and defence spending to support industries such as aerospace, brings with it some disadvantages for the rest of the economy. There may be low civilian spillovers from such R&D expenditure (Kaldor et al., 1986), and with the end of the Cold War these sectors have become increasingly vulnerable to cut-backs. To summarize, there appear to be grounds for concern over UK non-price competitiveness, particularly in the area of skills and innovation.[7] The importance of differences in technology as a factor affecting trade performance, shown by the earlier chapters, highlights the significance of these weaknesses to British competitiveness.

6.3 THE EMPIRICAL MODEL

The empirical analysis presented here aims to assess the importance of different determinants of trade performance, in particular innovation, and their variation across the two groups of innovating and non-innovating firms. There is increasing consensus in the literature on international trade that no single factor can neatly account for the trade patterns of developed countries. As a result, the empirical model considered here encompasses a number of different explanations for export performance. The explanatory variables used reflect both firm characteristics and the characteristics of the sector in which the firm is operating. The general relationship is given by:

$$X = f(\text{firm characteristics, market size, innovation})$$

where X is an indication of firm-level export performance, taken to be a function of firm characteristics, including capital intensity and average labour costs, firm size and the quadratic term for size. In addition, market size is included to reflect the environment in which the firm is situated. Innovation is included as a separate characteristic; sector-level innovation variables show the innovative environment of the firm, and the level of potential innovation spillovers to the firm. When possible, firm-level innovation variables are also included.

Firm characteristics are used to give an indication of the attributes of the firm and the general level of firm competitiveness. The capital variable indicates the level of firm assets, including machinery and buildings, which *embody* past innovations as well as influencing the marginal cost of the output of the firm. As a result, a positive relationship between capital intensity and trade performance is expected, as it indicates a firm's capabilities and past innovation. One potentially contradictory effect is that capital-intense products, for example, cement, may also have high transport costs which provide a disincentive to export. Unfortunately, there are no data available on transportability; for the manufacturing industries used in this analysis it is assumed to be relatively unimportant.

Two labour-cost variables are included: one is unit labour costs which indicates productivity; the other is average wages which may indicate skill levels as well as labour costs. Unit labour costs are likely to have a negative impact on exports in cost-sensitive export markets. For the average wage variable, a high average wage may indicate a firm with a large degree of accumulated human capital; this implies that the coefficient on the average salary variable might be positive. As Penrose (1958) argued, the competitive advantage of firms is fundamentally based on the cumulative and incremental learning of the firm's management, which subsequently differentiates firms from each other. Technological capabilities are embodied in firms and the people who work for them (Teece, 1986). There is considerable evidence for the importance of skills in determining the export performance of developed countries at a more aggregate level (Oulton, 1996). As the salary variable broken down by skill level is not available in this data set, the two variables, unit labour costs and average wages, are included to proxy costs and skills, respectively.

Firm size is expected to have a positive relationship to exports as larger firms have more resources with which to enter foreign markets. This may be particularly the case if there are fixed costs to exporting such as gathering information or covering the uncertainty of a foreign market. There may also be economies of production and marketing which benefit large firms. Clearly the importance of firm size can be expected to vary with the characteristics of the sector, such as the importance of economies of scale in the sector.

In addition, the square of firm size is used to test for non-linearities in the relationship between size and exports. It is possible that a minimum size is required to overcome the additional costs of exporting, beyond which increases in size have no impact on export performance. There are a number of studies which include such non-linearities; for instance, Kumar and

Siddharthan (1994) and Willmore (1992), both find a negative relationship for the quadratic term of size in the context of developing countries. The argument is that although size is an advantage in exporting, this may not apply to very large firms which may be more orientated towards the domestic market because of, for example, a domestic monopoly giving them no incentive to export. A firm faced with a domestic monopoly can exploit domestic demand; a foreign market would typically have a higher elasticity of demand, and would involve the domestic firm becoming a price taker. Following this hypothesis, the quadratic term of size is expected to have a negative coefficient.

In addition to the firm characteristics, industry-level variables are also included to account for the environment within which the firm operates. Domestic market size is included as firms located in sectors with large domestic markets are considered less likely to export in order to acquire the minimum efficient size. For the UK a reasonably large domestic market is available, although in some sectors (such as aerospace) very large economies of scale indicate that no domestic market alone can sustain the industry. Depending on the sector under consideration, we would expect a large domestic market to be negatively related to the probability of exporting (Glejser et al., 1980).

Finally, innovation variables – both at a sectoral level showing the innovation potential of the sector, and at a firm level giving the innovatory history of the firm – are expected to have a positive relationship to export performance. At the firm level, innovations are one indicator of a firm's competitiveness; innovations give firms an advantage over their competitors, and we would expect them to have a positive impact on exports. At the sector level, the innovation variables indicate the importance of an innovative environment (shown by the number of innovations produced and used) on the export performance of the firm, including the influence of spillovers from other firms. The innovations produced in each sector is an indication of the technological opportunity available in the sector, while innovations used show the level of innovation spillovers from the rest of the economy to that sector. A positive coefficient would indicate the importance of the innovative environment in influencing the exporting patterns of firms.

To summarize, a firm's propensity to export is expected to be influenced by firm-specific competitive advantages such as a high capital intensity, a skilled labour force and innovations. Market and firm structure are also expected to influence exports, and in particular the probability of a firm exporting, which is likely to be positively related to firm size and negatively to the size of the domestic market. The innovation level of the sector in which the firm is located is also expected to have a positive effect on firm exports.

6.4 THE DATA SET

The data set used in this chapter is a microeconomic data set of UK firms which covers just over 500 firms for a period of five years from 1988–92 and accounts for 67 per cent of total UK manufacturing output over the five years.[8] The data set involves a combination of information from the SPRU survey of major UK innovations with additional balance sheet data available from various sources. Until now the SPRU survey, which is a unique source of information on UK innovations, has been used either on its own (Pavitt et al., 1987 and Robson et al., 1988), or as an innovation proxy in macroeconomic studies (Greenhalgh, 1990), but has rarely been combined with additional firm-level data (see Geroski and Machin, 1993 for one example using only quoted firms). The data set used here aims to maintain the richness of the SPRU survey by considering a representative subsample of the firms surveyed. Given the number of firms covered by the survey it was necessary to consider only a subsample; however, the sample was not limited only to quoted firms but also includes non-quoted firms, an unusual feature of the data set because of the extra cost and difficulty in obtaining data on non-quoted firms. Smaller firms, which are often non-quoted, are a valuable and potentially underestimated source of innovation. Innovation studies, which count innovations produced, can counteract the tendency of R&D expenditure indicators to underestimate the contribution of small firms (see, for instance, Pavitt et al., 1987). Because of the Schumpeterian emphasis on the importance of large firms as dynamic sources of innovation, many studies of innovation have considered only the largest firms often in the US (Scherer, 1965; Simonetti, 1994). The survey tried to cover the spectrum of firm size and the sample used here has attempted to maintain that diversity. In this data set, 30 per cent of the sample of innovations came from firms with fewer than 500 employees.[9] The data set consists of two subsamples; the first sample is taken from the SPRU innovation survey and is described in the following subsection.

6.4.1 The Innovation Survey

The SPRU innovation data are from a survey of all the significant technical UK innovations which occurred from 1945 to 1983; the objective of the survey was to be exhaustive and cover the entire population of UK innovations. A survey was sent out to firms requesting information on their innovation history; in addition, a panel of experts was used to select the innovations and, wherever possible, their selection was confirmed with the relevant firm. The survey covered more than 4,000 individual innovations produced by 1,845 firms, and also includes extensive information on the innovations. The definition used for the inclusion of an innovation in the survey was 'the successful commercial introduction of new or improved products, processes or materials'. As a result, these innovations do not reflect all inventive activity, but only successful inventive activity, and can be interpreted as showing only the 'winners' from the risky process of invention. If we consider that inventors do not have complete information and are involved in a search process for successful inventions, while a number will succeed and discover inventions which have an economic value, there are also those inventions which are not implemented and have no economic significance. The latter are not considered by the survey. One weakness of direct counts of innovations is that each innovation is given equal weight, although the economic significance of the innovations varies greatly.

As part of the additional information given in the survey, firms were asked to respond to the question: 'Was the UK introduction of the innovation the first in the world?'. Only a subsample of the firms surveyed responded to this question; presumably those that did not answer did not have the relevant information. The firms which responded to this question were taken as a subsample, assuming that there is no selection bias between those that responded to the question and the rest of the survey, but that this subsample is representative of the population of innovators considered by the survey. Out of these firms only those in manufacturing sectors[10] were then chosen. As Pavitt et al. (1987) point out, 90 per cent of the innovations were commercialized by firms with their principal activity in manufacturing, so this selection covers the majority of innovations and excludes those activities which are not exportable. Those sources not considered are mainly research laboratories and large public utilities, neither of which are concerned with the export market of interest to this study. In order to decide for which unit of the firm to collect data, the status of the firm was considered. For those innovating units which had parent firms in the UK the parent firm was taken as the relevant unit of analysis, in order to simplify data collection. For those firms which are subsidiaries of foreign firms the UK subsidiary was considered as the unit of analysis; for all other firms the issue was not relevant.

Using this subsample of respondents as the sample of innovating firms, additional data were then obtained from two separate sources for the quoted firms and the non-quoted firms (see the Appendix for details of the sources). Not all the firms were found in the two data sources and in the end there were 214 firms (85 quoted, 129 non-quoted) as part of the innovating sample. The sample firms are responsible for 658 innovations, about 15 per cent of the total innovations recorded by the survey.

6.4.2 The Non-innovators

The second group of firms was chosen randomly from the same two data sources. The ratio between quoted and non-quoted firms was taken from the sample of innovators, that is, approximately one-third quoted to two-thirds non-quoted firms. A random number generator was used to choose which firms were to be selected; again, the firms were restricted to manufacturing industries but the status of the firm was not known in advance. As this sample reflects the population of firms covered by the two data sources, there may be innovating firms (firms from the survey) included in the sample. In the case of the quoted firms the data source is comprehensive, including all quoted firms which have published their first year's trading results. The coverage is very extensive in the case of non-quoted firms.[11] The firms were then screened for innovators (firms included in the survey) which were then discarded. The remaining firms are classified as non-innovators. A similar number of firms was collected for the non-innovators' as for the innovators' sample, approximately 290.

The data for each firm are for five years from 1988 to 1992 inclusive, providing a short panel. This period is considerably later than that covered by the innovation survey, which is for the period 1945–83, and so relies on the longevity of the impact of the innovations, or rather the continuing status of these firms as innovators (and of the other firms as non-innovators). In order to control for this the year of the commercial introduction of the innovation is also considered; clearly innovations from the late 1940s and 50s may no longer be having any significant economic impact on the performance of the firm. The industry classification and status (independent or subsidiary) are known for each firm, and aggregate innovation variables can also be made for each industry from the survey. The firm innovation data are aggregated to give variables for innovations produced in that industry and innovations used in the industry.

The data set is a rich one and can be divided into two groups based on the innovation characteristics of the firms, namely innovators and non-innovators. There are two points about the data which should be taken into account. The first is that for the sample of innovating firms data were collected for the UK parent firm where relevant; in contrast, the non-innovating firms were chosen without considering their status. This is not expected to be a problem, as the lack of data on subsidiaries in the data source prompted the use of the parent firms in the first place; as a result, many of the firms chosen randomly are likely to be parent firms. Nevertheless, the calculations should control for firm size which may be larger on average for the innovators because of the choice of parent companies rather than as a result of their status as innovators.

Foreign ownership cannot be identified in the random sample, which classifies firms as either independent or a subsidiary without any information on the nationality of the parent company; this information is available for the firms taken from the survey.

The second point is that the export variable for quoted firms includes sales to overseas subsidiaries. This is due to changes in accounting methods: exports are no longer reported directly but rather total sales and domestic sales are reported separately and the difference between the two is taken to represent exports but includes, in addition, sales to overseas subsidiaries. This is not the case for the non-quoted firms, which are asked to report exports directly. This difference affects the two groups of innovating and non-innovating firms in the same way, and as a result does not introduce a bias between these two groups. As far as this chapter is concerned, the inclusion of sales to overseas subsidiaries with exports is not problematic; innovation should be an important factor affecting both intra-firm and inter-firm trade.[12]

The definitions of the main variables available in the data set are given below, followed by some descriptive statistics, in order to highlight some general differences between the two groups. Some variables are available at the firm level while others are at the sector level. All the variables considered are available for both groups of firms.

6.4.3 Descriptive Statistics

Each of the variables defined below is available annually for the period 1988 to 1992:

propensity to export: $PX_f = X_f \,/\, TS_f$;

average capital intensity:[13] $KSA_f = TK_f \,/\, TS_f$;

average wages: $AS_f = TR_f \,/\, SIZE_f$;

unit labour costs: $ULC_f = TR_f \,/\, TS_f$;

share of UK output: $MP_f = TS_f \,/\, SEC$;

where X stands for exports, TS for total sales, TK for total capital, $SIZE$ for the number of employees, TR for total remuneration, and the subscript f is for the firm. SEC is total sales in the sector in which the firm is located defined at the two-digit 1980 SIC level.[14] The explanatory variables are scaled either by an indicator of firm size, such as the number of employees, total firm sales, or by the number of enterprises in the sector if they are at a sectoral level. As Deardorff (1984) points out, scaling is important in reducing heteroscedasticity. The different innovation variables available are:

USER – the number of innovations used in the sector from 1979–83, taken from the SPRU survey, scaled by the number of enterprises in the sector;

PROD – the number of innovations produced in the sector for 1979–83, from the survey, excluding each firm's individual innovations, scaled by the number of enterprises in the sector;

R&D – the expenditure on R&D in the sector, excluding each firm's R&D expenditure, scaled by the number of enterprises in the sector;

INPER – the number of innovations of the firm for the period of the survey;

RD_f – firm–level R&D expenditure for each year scaled by total firm sales.

The first three innovation variables are at a sector level and the last two at the firm level. The problem with the firm level innovation variables is that *INPER* is only available for the innovating firms, and therefore cannot be used in the model which separates the firms into two groups, while firm-level R&D is only available for the quoted firms. As a result when the whole sample is used only sector-level innovation variables are included.

The number of firms that export in this sample varies considerably between the two groups. For the innovating firms 49 per cent of the firms export, while for the non-innovating firms the proportion falls to 38 per cent, indicating that innovating firms are more likely to enter export markets than non-innovating firms. Some descriptive statistics are given in Table 6.1 for the two separate classifications of innovators and non-innovators. They are taken as averages across the five years for each of the variables.

The first important point from Table 6.1 is that the innovating firms have a higher propensity to export than the non-innovating firms (almost 50 per cent higher), giving some aggregate evidence that innovation has a positive impact on export performance at the firm level. When non-exporting firms are excluded and the propensity to export of the exporting firms alone is considered, the difference between innovators and non-innovators remains; this implies that innovation has a positive impact on export behaviour at the firm. This is consistent with the comparison made in Hirsch and Bijaoui (1985), when they contrasted the propensity to export of a group of innovating firms (firms with R&D programmes) relative to the average in each sector. They found that their sample of innovating firms were exporting more than indicated by the sector average.

Table 6.1 Descriptive statistics

	Innovators		Non-innovators	
	mean	s.d.	mean	s.d.
Propensity to export – all firms	0.29	0.31	0.20	0.28
Propensity to export – exporters	0.45	0.27	0.33	0.29
Average capital intensity	0.44	0.36	0.43	0.91
Unit labour costs	0.22	0.16	0.23	0.15
Average remuneration (£)	14,104	4,567	11,765	4,472
Number of firm innovations	3.08	6.95	–	–
UK output share	0.05	0.13	0.01	0.04
Number of employees	10,360	22,774	3,259	14,532
Innovations produced in the sector	532	422	353	405
Innovations used in the sector	290	184	211	187
R&D at the sector (£ million)	633	672	464	664

The most dramatic difference across the two groups is given by variations in firm size, shown by both the output share variable and the number of employees. The output share variable for the innovators has a mean five times that of the non-innovators. This variation is consistent with Geroski and Machin (1993), who also found the market share of innovating firms in their sample to be almost five times higher than the non-innovating firms in the sample. Their sample differed from that used here as it consisted only of quoted firms. However, despite this, the difference in the mean output share between the innovators and non-innovators is very similar to that found here. While the output share index is based on sales, the number of employees also attests to important differences in firm size. The innovating firms are on average more than three times the average size of non-innovating firms based on the number of employees. The standard deviation of the distribution of the number of employees is also very high in each of the groups, indicating that firm size still varies considerably within the groups as well as between them. Thus there appear to be important differences in size between innovating and non-innovating firms. The use of means to summarize the data may disguise the complexity of the relationship between innovation and firm size. Pavitt et al. (1987) found a U-shaped relationship between innovation and firm size, with small specialized firms very active in innovation, along with large firms exploiting the possibilities of R&D-based diversification into other product markets. Nevertheless, the descriptive evidence considered here points to an increasing relationship between firm size and innovation, with innovating firms being characterized by higher-than-average size when contrasted with non-innovating firms.

The number of innovations per firm indicates that the innovators had, on average, just over three per firm; the high standard deviation indicates a great deal of variety between the different firms. The innovators also operate in sectors which produce and use more innovations, and spend more on R&D, than the sectors in which the non-innovating firms are located, so innovating firms are located in sectors in which the opportunity to innovate is higher, as we would expect.

The non-innovating sample has a higher ratio of non-quoted firms to quoted firms than the innovating sample, which may partly explain the lower mean of this group. In order to control for this and examine differences across quoted and non-quoted firms, Table 6.2 gives the descriptive statistics for the same groups as Table 6.1, separated into the two subgroups of quoted and non-quoted firms; the standard deviations are in brackets.

The probability of exporting also varies for the innovating and non-innovating firms when they are divided into quoted and non-quoted. For the quoted firms, 74 per cent of the innovators export, while for the non-innovators the proportion is 64 per cent. As far as the non-quoted firms are concerned, 32 per cent of the innovators export compared with 28 per cent of the non-innovators.

The difference between the propensity to export for innovators with respect to the non-innovating firms is also clear for both the quoted and non-quoted firms. The quoted innovators export on average about half their total sales, while the non-innovators export about a third. Considering only the non-quoted firms which export, the propensity to export is higher for the innovators (35 per cent) than for the non-innovators (28 per cent). Again, these descriptive statistics confirm that innovating firms are more likely to export, and when they are exporters, they export a higher proportion of output; this relationship appears to be influenced by size, with the difference between innovators and non-innovators being more apparent for the quoted than for the non-quoted firms.

The size difference between the innovating and non-innovating firms is very clear for the quoted and non-quoted firms. It is the difference between the mean number of employees for the non-quoted firms which is the most dramatic. The mean for the non-quoted innovators is eleven times larger than for the non-innovating non-quoted firms, while for the quoted firms the same ratio is just over two. Likewise, for the output share variable the quoted innovating firms have on average more than three times the output share of the quoted non-innovators; for the non-quoted firms the same ratio is twenty.

Table 6.2 Descriptive statistics for quoted and non-quoted firms

	Innovators		Non-innovators	
	quoted	non-quoted	quoted	non-quoted
Propensity to export – all firms	0.49 (0.26)	0.15 (0.25)	0.31 (0.30)	0.14 (0.25)
Propensity to export – exporters	0.51 (0.25)	0.35 (0.28)	0.37 (0.29)	0.28 (0.29)
Average capital intensity	0.54 (0.28)	0.37 (0.39)	0.68 (0.61)	0.30 (1.00)
Unit labour costs	0.22 (0.08)	0.22 (0.20)	0.21 (0.10)	0.23 (0.12)
Average remuneration (£)	14,055 (3,261)	14,140 (5,330)	11,684 (3,722)	11,806 (4,806)
Number of firm innovations	5.22 (10.29)	1.70 (2.34)	–	–
UK output share	0.10 (0.18)	0.02 (0.07)	0.03 (0.06)	0.001 (0.003)
Number of employees	21,312 (30,498)	2,254 (7,785)	9,350 (24,012)	200 (532)
Innovations produced in the sector	513 (420)	545 (423)	311 (387)	370 (412)
Innovations used in the sector	299 (187)	285 (183)	199 (185)	216 (118)
R&D for the sector (£ million)	693 (702)	594 (649)	464 (650)	464 (669)

Average capital intensity appears to vary across the quoted and non-quoted firms rather than across innovators and non-innovators. The latter also appear to be characterized by a high degree of heterogeneity within the non-innovating groups, shown by the high standard deviations. As far as innovation is concerned, the quoted innovators have on average more than five innovations each, although there is also a great deal of variation within this group as shown by the high standard deviation: the number of innovations per non-quoted firm is less than two. For the sector-level innovation variables, the innovating firms come from sectors which produced and used more innovations and had higher R&D expenditure than non-innovating firms for both quoted and non-quoted groups. As already indicated by Table 6.1, innovative firms come from sectors with higher average levels of innovation.

To summarize, the most important differences between the groups are in terms of export behaviour – both the propensity to export and the probability of exporting – and firm size, shown either by output share or by the number of employees. The propensity to export is much higher for the innovating firms than for the non-innovating firms, and innovating firms are more likely to export than non-innovators, lending support to the hypothesis that trade performance is significantly affected by innovation. On average the innovating firms are significantly larger than the non-innovating firms, indicating a strong relationship between firm size and innovation. The most important result for the ensuing analysis is the need to separate the impact of firm size on exports from the impact of being an innovator. The quoted firms could also be examined as a subsample, as the impact on exports appears to be particularly important for this group. In general, the role of an innovative environment can be seen from the higher average sectoral R&D and innovations produced and used in sectors where innovating firms are found. The two groups of firms appear to have important differences between them, suggesting that different factors may determine export performance for the different groups.

6.5 THE RESULTS

6.5.1 The Choice of Specification

In the data set there are a number of firms which have no exports, thus the dependent variable frequently takes a value of zero. The propensity to export is taken as the dependent variable indicating export performance; it varies between zero and one by definition. As a result, OLS regression may not be the most suitable estimation procedure, as it can give estimates which imply predictions of the propensity to export outside its possible range, that is, higher than one and lower than zero. In order to find the best model specification, two alternatives are tested against each other, following Cragg (1971). The first specification is to estimate a single censored model, termed a

Tobit model, which uses all the available information from the explanatory variables, including those for which the dependent variable is zero. However, the Tobit model is very restrictive as it includes both the decision of whether or not to export and the level of exports relative to sales in one model, that is, it imposes the same coefficients on the explanatory factors for the two decisions (see Lin and Schmidt, 1984, for details).

The alternative specification is to estimate two models, in order to separate the decision of whether or not to export from the decision of how much to export. The first uses the whole data set and considers the decision of whether or not to export. The dependent variable is binary, taking a value of one when the firm exports and zero when it does not; for this a probit model is appropriate, estimated by the maximum likelihood method. The model assumes an underlying Y^* which cannot be seen. Instead a variable Y can be observed which takes a value one when Y^* is more than zero, and zero when it is equal or less than zero. Y is taken from the export data, one if the firm has exports in a particular year and zero if it does not. For the second model only the subset of firms which export are considered and the relationship is estimated taking into account that the dependent variable cannot be zero or less and is therefore truncated; again, maximum likelihood estimation is used. The truncated model is different from the model considering the full sample, as the information on those data points for which the dependent variable is zero is not included. Thus the model does not include all the available information, but does allow the decision of how much to export to be estimated separately from the decision to export. This double specification can be tested as the unrestricted model against a Tobit model as the restricted model.

The unrestricted model is given below in equations (6.1) and (6.2). In equation (6.1) the dependent variable of the model is the probability of exporting Y which takes the value of one when a firm exports and zero when it does not and is estimated for all firms, in equation (6.2) it is the propensity to export, and is estimated only for the exporting firms:

$$
\begin{aligned}
Y = {} & \alpha + \beta_1 KSA + \beta_2 AS + \beta_3 SIZE + \beta_4 SIZE^2 + \beta_5 SEC \\
& + \beta_6 INN + \beta_7 ULC + \beta_8 DUM + \varepsilon_1
\end{aligned}
\tag{6.1}
$$

where $y = 1$ if $x > 0$, x is exports and $y = 0$ if $x = 0$.

For the firms for which $y = 1$ and the propensity to export is the dependent variable:

$$
\begin{aligned}
PX = {} & \delta + \gamma_1 KSA + \gamma_2 AS + \gamma_3 SIZE + \gamma_4 SIZE^2 + \gamma_5 SEC \\
& + \gamma_6 INN + \gamma_7 ULC + \gamma_8 DUM + \varepsilon_2
\end{aligned}
\tag{6.2}
$$

all the variables are as defined earlier, *INN* is one of the choice of innovation variables. For the restricted Tobit model, equation (6.2) is estimated for the whole sample. The results of the three models are given below in Table 6.3, with all the data pooled across years. The first column of the table gives the results for the Tobit censored model with the propensity to export as the dependent variable, the second column the probit model of the probability of exporting, while the third gives the truncated model for the propensity to export for the subset of exporting firms.

Table 6.3 Choice of specification

	Tobit $Y = PX$	Probit $Y = Y$	Truncated $Y = PX$
α	−0.16	−0.01	−0.61
	(0.04)***	(0.13)	(0.11)***
KSA	0.10	0.21	0.16
	(0.02)***	(0.07)***	(0.04)***
AS	0.02	0.02	0.03
	(0.002) ***	(0.008)***	(0.01)***
SIZE	$0.14 \ 10^{-4}$	$0.56 \ 10^{-4}$	$0.11 \ 10^{-4}$
	$(0.13 \ 10^{-5})$***	$(0.68 \ 10^{-5})$***	$(0.19 \ 10^{-5})$***
SIZE^2	$-0.81 \ 10^{-10}$	$-0.33 \ 10^{-9}$	$-0.58 \ 10^{-10}$
	$(0.11 \ 10^{-10})$***	$(0.56 \ 10^{-10})$***	$(0.16 \ 10^{-10})$***
USER	0.47	2.02	0.12
	(0.21)**	(0.76)***	(0.35)
SEC	$-0.51 \ 10^{-6}$	$-0.54 \ 10^{-5}$	$0.19 \ 10^{-5}$
	$(0.76 \ 10^{-6})$	$(0.25 \ 10^{-5})$**	$(0.14 \ 10^{-5})$
ULC	0.14	0.15	0.36
	(0.08)*	(0.26)	(0.19)**
DUM	−0.02	−0.23***	0.11
	(0.02)	(0.07)	(0.04)***

Notes:
Significant * at 10%, ** at 5%, *** at 1%.
σ Tobit = 0.37 (0.01), σ trunc = 0.38 (0.02).
Log likelihood: Tobit = −881.5, probit = −948.6, trunc = 99.8.

Taking the Tobit model as the restricted model, and the probit and truncated together as the unrestricted model, the Tobit model was rejected at 99 per cent probability using a chi-squared test with 6 degrees of freedom based on the likelihood ratio statistic given below (the test statistic was 65.4). Such a test is possible as the log likelihood functions for the second two tests together add up to the log likelihood function for the Tobit model (see Greene, 1993, for details). The test is given below:

$$\lambda = -2[\ln L_t - (\ln L_p + \ln L_{tr})]$$

where L_t is the likelihood for the Tobit model, L_p for the probit model and L_{tr} for the truncated model. The probit model correctly predicts 68 per cent of the outcomes from the model.

There appear to be important differences between the influence of the explanatory variables according to whether the probability of exporting or the propensity to export is considered.

1. *USER*, the number of innovations used in the sector, is positively and significantly related to the probability of exporting, and is positive but not significant for the propensity to export of the exporting firms.[15]
2. The coefficient on the sector size variable *SEC* also varies according to the model used. It appears to be negatively, and significantly, related to the probability of exporting and positively to the propensity to export. So a large domestic market appears to be a disincentive to export, but for the propensity to export there is a positive relationship between domestic market size and exports, indicating some relationship between market structure and the export behaviour of firms.

Firm characteristics are generally significant, with capital intensity and average salary both being positively related to exports. Unit labour costs are also positively related to exports, but are not significant for the probit model. This confirms the importance of firm-level competitive advantages in influencing exports, both innovations 'embodied' in capital and the skills of the workforce positively influence a firm's competitiveness on international markets. The *SIZE* variable is also positively significant for both models and the $SIZE^2$ negatively significant, indicating an inverted U-shaped relationship between firm size and exports (and the probability of exporting). This result confirms the results found for developing countries (India and Brazil), that there are important non-linearities in the relationship between size and exports.

The decision to pool the data across all five years was then tested using this specification procedure. Dummy variables were included for each of the four years from 1989 to 1992 and for both the intercept and all the explanatory variables with 1988 being left as the base year, R&D was taken as the innovation variable as it varies over time. None of the dummy variables, either for the intercept or for the explanatory variables, was significant. Thus there seem to be no significant differences over the five years, allowing the data to be pooled across years. To summarize, the two-fold estimation technique is favoured as being more appropriate in this case than a Tobit model, and as a result the decision to export and the propensity to export of those firms which export in the sample are estimated separately.

6.5.2 The Probability of Firms Exporting

Considering first the probit model for the probability of exporting, the separation of firms into innovative firms and non-innovating firms was tested to see if the probability of exporting or not exporting varies over the two groups. The restricted probit model is that given in line two of Table 6.3. The unrestricted model separates both the intercept and the explanatory variables into the two different groups. A chi-squared test was then made for the unrestricted model relative to the restricted model, following the test outlined above. The restriction was rejected at 99 per cent confidence level, indicating that the innovating firms should be estimated separately from the non-innovating firms. These models were re-estimated with two alternative innovation variables: *PROD* the number of innovations produced in the sector, and *R&D* the level of R&D expenditure in the sector. For each of these innovation variables the restricted model was rejected relative to the model separating the non-innovating from the innovating firms. The results are given in Table 6.4.

There are four main differences between the results for the innovating and non-innovating firms and they refer to the innovation, labour, capital intensity and domestic market size variables. The differences are outlined below.

1. For all three innovation variables, the coefficients are positively significant for the non-innovating group and positive but not significant for the innovating firms (with the exception of the use of innovations which is just significant at 10 per cent). While being in an industry which produces and uses a large number of innovations and has high R&D expenditure significantly increases the probability of non-innovating firms exporting, it has much less effect on the innovating firms.

2. Unit labour costs are negatively related to the probability of exporting for the non-innovating firms, indicating that cost considerations play some role in their export performance. Average wages are positive, indicating a possible skill effect which is separate from the advantages of low unit labour costs. For innovating firms, there are opposite signs on the two labour variables. Unit labour costs are positively related to the probability of exporting, while average wages are not significant. This positive sign

Table 6.4 The unrestricted probit models

	α	KSA	AS	SIZE	SIZE^2	INN	ULC	SEC
Innovators								
USER	-0.25	0.39***	-0.01	$0.8\ 10^{-4}$***	$-0.5\ 10^{-9}$***	2.05*	0.94**	$0.3\ 10^{-5}$
	(0.23)	(0.15)	(0.01)	$(0.1\ 10^{-4})$	$(0.9\ 10^{-10})$	(1.12)	(0.47)	$(0.4\ 10^{-5})$
PROD	-0.31	0.41***	-0.01	$0.8\ 10^{-4}$***	$-0.5\ 10^{-9}$***	1.17	0.85*	$0.4\ 10^{-5}$
	(0.24)	(0.15)	(0.01)	$(0.1\ 10^{-4})$	$(0.9\ 10^{-10})$	(0.77)	(0.47)	$(0.5\ 10^{-5})$
R&D	-0.20	0.39***	-0.01	$0.8\ 10^{-4}$***	$-0.5\ 10^{-9}$***	0.34	0.89**	$0.2\ 10^{-5}$
	(0.23)	(0.14)	(0.01)	$(0.1\ 10^{-4})$	$(0.9\ 10^{-10})$	(0.25)	(0.47)	$(0.4\ 10^{-5})$
Non-innovators								
USER	-0.08	0.14*	0.06***	$0.3\ 10^{-4}$***	$-0.2\ 10^{-9}$**	3.49***	-0.63*	$-0.1\ 10^{-4}$***
	(0.18)	(0.09)	(0.01)	$(0.1\ 10^{-4})$	$(0.1\ 10^{-9})$	(1.15)	(0.39)	$(0.3\ 10^{-5})$
PROD	-0.10	0.15*	0.06***	$0.3\ 10^{-4}$***	$-0.2\ 10^{-9}$**	3.36***	-0.70*	$-0.1\ 10^{-4}$***
	(0.16)	(0.09)	(0.01)	$(0.1\ 10^{-4})$	$(0.1\ 10^{-9})$	(0.95)	(0.38)	$(0.3\ 10^{-5})$
R&D	-0.10**	0.17*	0.06***	$0.3\ 10^{-4}$***	$-0.2\ 10^{-9}$**	1.60***	-0.63*	$-0.1\ 10^{-4}$***
	(0.18)	(0.09)	(0.01)	$(0.1\ 10^{-4})$	$(0.8\ 10^{-10})$	(0.34)	(0.40)	$(0.3\ 10^{-5})$

Notes: * Significant at 10%, **significant at 5%, *** at 1%, McFadden's R^2: for USER = 0.10, PROD = 0.10, R&D = 0.11, Log likelihood: USER = -924.1; PROD = -923.3; R&D = -916.9.

may indicate that innovating firms export higher-quality goods which are less price sensitive.

3. The impact of the capital intensity variable on export behaviour is much larger for the innovating firms than for the non-innovating firms, as can be seen from the much larger coefficients on the capital intensity variable for the innovating firms. This indicates the role of past innovations in the capital equipment of the innovating firms. Firms which have innovated appear to be more capital intense, which in turn makes them more likely to export.

4. The domestic market size variable *SEC*, is negative and significant for the non-innovating sample of firms, but positive and not significant for the innovating firms, indicating that non-innovating firms in smaller domestic markets are more likely to export. However, for the innovating firms the probability of exporting does not appear to be affected by domestic market size. This could be an indication that market characteristics are less important for innovative firms, who export because of the innovative nature of their product, not in response to domestic market structure.

The three models have the same percentage of correct predictions at 70 per cent, the pseudo R^2 are also very similar, and no one sector technology variable appears to explain more of the dependent variable than any other.

The most important result is that the two sets of firms, innovators and non-innovators appear to behave differently. This may be due directly to the accumulated economic benefits of the individual innovations themselves, or that innovating firms have some generic differences from non-innovators, such as better management. Size is certainly one factor, as we have seen from the descriptive statistics, the innovating firms are significantly larger on average than the non-innovating firms. However, even taking account of size, as in this specification, there still appear to be differences in the export behaviour of the two groups of firms. Innovating firms have different determinants for the probability of exporting which cannot just be explained by their difference in size. This is consistent with the results of Geroski and Machin (1993), which showed that the determinants of profits varies between innovating and non-innovating firms.

The importance of the sector-level innovation variables for the non-innovating firms also indicates that the innovation environment is important for those firms which rely on other firms in the economy for their innovations, but less important for the innovating firms which can rely on their own innovative capabilities. The importance of the innovation variables for the non-innovating UK firms indicates that innovation does play an important part in firms' trade performance. It is interesting to note that despite the differences in the formulations of the sector–level innovation variables, the results in Table 6.4 are not sensitive to which is used.

6.5.3 The Propensity of Firms to Export

The second model, for the propensity of the exporting firms alone to export, was then estimated using all three innovation variables. The restricted model estimating both the innovating and non-innovating firms together in Table 6.3, was rejected relative to the unrestricted models in all three cases, again indicating significant differences between the two groups of firms. The results for the three unrestricted models are given in Table 6.5.

For this model considering the propensity of the exporting firms to export, there are important differences in the capital intensity, unit labour costs, $SIZE^2$ and innovation variables for the two groups of survey and non-innovating firms.

1. The capital intensity variable, KSA, is positively and significantly related to exports for the innovating firms, but is not significant for the non-innovating firms. It appears that capital intensity increases the probability of exporting for the non-innovating firms, but it has no significant effect on the propensity to export. That it is positively significant for the innovating firms indicates the relationship between capital and innovation. Much technical change is embedded in capital equipment, so that capital embodies past innovations, and thus increases the propensity to export.
2. The quadratic term of the size variable is negative for both the groups but not significantly so for the non-innovators. Unlike in the probit model already discussed, the negative relationship between increasing size and the level of exports affects innovatory firms more than non-innovators. Overall, however, the inverted U-shaped relationship between exports and firm size can still be seen.
3. Unlike the probit model, the choice of innovation variable affects the results. The production of innovations ($PROD$) is positive for both groups but significant only for the non-innovators, while sector R&D expenditure is negative for both and significantly so for the innovative firms. This result for R&D expenditure may indicate rivalry between different firms' R&D expenditure. Overall, the level of exports of the exporting firms in the non-innovators to be favourably related to innovation spillovers from within the sector ($PROD$),[16] for the innovating spillovers seem to have little effect on their trade performance. The sensitivity of the results to the innovation variable used indicates that the results of studies which rely exclusively on R&D data (such as Hirsch and Bijaoui, 1985, and Kumar

Table 6.5 The unrestricted truncated models

	α	KSA	AS	SIZE	$SIZE^2$	INN	ULC
Innovators							
USER	−0.23***	0.36***	0.02***	$0.1\,10^{-4}$***	$-0.5\,10^{-10}$***	−0.06	0.37**
	(0.08)	(0.06)	(0.01)	$(0.1\,10^{-5})$	$(0.1\,10^{-10})$	(0.29)	(0.16)
PROD	−0.24***	0.36***	0.02***	$0.1\,10^{-4}$***	$-0.5\,10^{-10}$***	0.19	0.39**
	(0.08)	(0.05)	(0.004)	$(0.1\,10^{-5})$	$(0.1\,10^{-10})$	(0.21)	(0.16)
R&D	−0.23***	0.38***	0.02***	$0.1\,10^{-4}$***	$-0.5\,10^{-10}$***	−0.14**	0.33**
	(0.08)	(0.05)	(0.004)	$(0.1\,10^{-5})$	$(0.1\,10^{-9})$	(0.07)	(0.16)
Non-innovators							
USER	−1.63***	0.11	0.08***	$0.2\,10^{-4}$***	$-0.5\,10^{-10}$	0.92	−0.46
	(0.51)	(0.11)	(0.02)	$(0.7\,10^{-5})$	$(0.5\,10^{-10})$	(1.19)	(0.57)
PROD	−1.66***	0.12	0.08***	$0.2\,10^{-4}$***	$-0.4\,10^{-10}$	3.35***	−0.38
	(0.48)	(0.12)	(0.02)	$(0.6\,10^{-5})$	$(0.4\,10^{-10})$	(1.09)	(0.53)
R&D	−1.60***	0.10	0.08***	$0.2\,10^{-4}$***	$-0.5\,10^{-10}$	−0.02	−0.49
	(0.51)	(0.11)	(0.02)	$(0.7\,10^{-5})$	$(0.5\,10^{-10})$	(0.32)	(0.57)

Notes:
σ USER = 0.60 (0.07) σ PROD = 0.57 (0.06) σ R&D = 0.59 (0.07). Log likelihood: USER, LL = 120.1; PROD, LL = 127.6; R&D, LL = 121.3.

146

and Siddharthan, 1994) may differ from those presented here and in other papers using actual innovation counts.

4. While the average wage variable is positively related to exports for both groups of firms, there is a noticeable difference in the unit labour-cost variable. The latter is positive and significant for the innovating firms, and negative and not significant for the non-innovators. One explanation for this result is that innovating firms export higher-quality goods and are thus less likely to be adversely affected by high unit labour costs. The results for the unit labour-cost variable are consistent with those for the probability of exporting. In both models, unit labour costs are negatively related to export behaviour for the non-innovators, and positively for the innovators. This indicates an important difference between innovating and non-innovating firms. Although the descriptive statistics in Table 6.1 indicate that both groups of firms have similar average unit labour costs, in the case of innovating firms it is the firms with higher unit labour costs which are more likely to export and which have a higher propensity to export. The opposite is true for the non-innovating firms.

To summarize, the models give some consistent results. Innovating firms should be estimated separately from the non-innovating firms, as the determinants of the probability of exporting and the propensity to export vary significantly for these firms. Firm characteristics are important in influencing exports. Firm size is positively related to the propensity to export for both groups of firms. Unit labour costs have a negative effect on non-innovating firms' export behaviour, but have a positive one on innovating firms' exports, indicating that the former are more price sensitive than the latter. Being an innovator reduces the probability of exporting, but raises the propensity to export, indicating that once firms export, innovations are likely to improve firm performance. Capital intensity is positively related both to the probability of exporting, and to the propensity of the exporters to export, although the latter is more important for the innovating firms.

As far as sector-specific characteristics are concerned, the size of the domestic market negatively affects non-innovating firms, which are less likely to export given a large domestic market. The size of the domestic market is not significant in the case of the innovating firms, for whom the probability of exporting appears to be based on firm, rather than sector, characteristics. The innovative environment of the firms is positively related to exports for the non-innovating firms but not particularly for the innovators, indicating that overall for non-innovating firms, spillovers of innovations are important either within the sector or from other sectors. The importance of such spillovers is not so relevant for the innovating firms themselves, however, as they can afford to be self-sufficient on their own innovations.

In order to consider the relationship for an important subgroup of firms, the model is now estimated for the quoted firms alone. This sample also has the benefit that firm-level R&D expenditure is available for these firms, so that the relationship between firm-level and sector-level innovation can be investigated for this group of firms.

6.6 QUOTED FIRM BEHAVIOUR

Because of the considerable variation in size across the different groups of firms, it is interesting to take a more homogeneous subsample of firms, in this case all quoted firms, and consider the determinants of trade performance for them alone. As the descriptive statistics showed, although there are still differences in size between innovating and non-innovating quoted firms, the largest differences are to be seen for the non-quoted firms. This section uses firm R&D expenditure as a proxy for firm-level innovation; this proxy is more satisfactory in the case of large firms, which are likely to have an R&D budget, than it is in the case of small firms which may undertake less formal R&D but still innovate.

In addition to the other variables, firm-level R&D expenditure is included in the model as RD_f which is firm-level R&D scaled by total firm sales. All the quoted firms in the sample were taken, giving 170 quoted firms. Of these firms, only 14 are non-exporters, that is, 8 per cent of the sample; this is considerably smaller than the proportion of non-exporters in the total sample, which is 25 per cent. As a result, the test of the separation into two stages for the probability of exporting and the propensity to export, against the Tobit model, was repeated for the quoted firms.

Once again the Tobit model was rejected, so the dual estimation technique outlined earlier is also applied for the quoted firms alone. As only a small number of firms in this sample do not export, the decision of whether or not to export is of less interest. As a result, only the truncated model taking the exports of the exporting firms alone is considered. The separation into innovators and non-innovating firms was tested. The restricted model estimating the two groups of firms together was rejected, indicating that in the case of the quoted firms the two groups should also be separated. The model is repeated for all three innovation proxies.[17] The results are presented in Table 6.6.

Table 6.6 Quoted firm results for the truncated model

	α	KSA	AS	SIZE	$SIZE^2$	RD_f	INN	ULC
Innovators								
USER	-0.19 **	0.35 ***	0.03 ***	$0.54\ 10^{-5}$ ***	$-0.40\ 10^{-10}$ ***	0.83 *	-0.003	0.15
	(0.08)	(0.06)	(0.004)	$(0.12\ 10^{-5})$	$(0.97\ 10^{-11})$	(0.46)	(0.26)	(0.19)
PROD	-0.19 **	0.36 ***	0.03 ***	$0.53\ 10^{-5}$ ***	$-0.39\ 10^{-10}$ ***	0.86 **	-0.05	0.03
	(0.08)	(0.06)	(0.004)	$(0.12\ 10^{-5})$	$(0.98\ 10^{-1})$	(0.47)	(0.22)	(0.17)
R&D	-0.17 **	0.37 ***	0.03 ***	$0.52\ 10^{-5}$ ***	$-0.36\ 10^{-10}$ ***	1.06 **	-0.17***	0.06
	(0.08)	(0.05)	(0.004)	$(0.12\ 10^{-5})$	$(0.96\ 10^{-11})$	(0.46)	(0.06)	(0.17)
Non-innovators								
USER	-0.64 ***	-0.04	0.07 ***	$0.67\ 10^{-5}$ ***	$-0.27\ 10^{-11}$	1.63	1.09	-0.94***
	(0.19)	(0.07)	(0.01)	$(0.33\ 10^{-5})$	$(0.24\ 10^{-10})$	(1.93)	(0.71)	(0.36)
PROD	-0.66 ***	-0.03	0.07 ***	$0.73\ 10^{-5}$ **	$-0.22\ 10^{-11}$	1.18	1.44 **	-0.93***
	(0.19)	(0.07)	(0.01)	$(0.33\ 10^{-5})$	$(0.24\ 10^{-10})$	(1.97)	(0.78)	(0.36)
R&D	-0.62 ***	0.04	0.07***	$0.72\ 10^{-5}$**	$-0.36\ 10^{-11}$	1.32	0.22	-0.98***
	(0.19)	(0.07)	(0.01)	$(0.33\ 10^{-5})$	$(0.24\ 10^{-10})$	(2.17)	(0.22)	(0.36)

Notes:
Innovators: σ USER = 0.21 (0.01) ***, LL = 63.8; σ PROD = 0.21 (0.01) ***, LL = 63.8; σ R&D = 0.21 (0.01)***, LL = 67.8.
Non-innovators: σ USER = 0.36 (0.03) ***, LL = 48.0; σ PROD = 0.36 (0.03) ***, LL = 48.6; σ R&D = 0.36 (0.03) ***, LL = 47.4.

The variable of most interest is firm-level R&D expenditure. This is positive and significant in the case of the innovating firms' propensity to export, and not significant for the non-innovating firms. So firm-level R&D has a particular effect for the innovating firms' propensity to export. While about half of the firms in the survey sample undertake R&D expenditure, only a quarter of the non-innovating firms do; thus innovating firms undertake significantly greater R&D expenditure. The greater impact of R&D expenditure on the innovators implies the importance of firm characteristics in affecting the performance of innovating firms. If we take R&D expenditure as indicative of firm-level innovation (as an input into the process of innovation) then it appears that innovative firms rely more on their own innovative capacity than the non-innovating firms, which seem to be influenced by the level of innovation in the sector, even in the case where they have an R&D budget.

For the non-innovating firms the sector innovation variable (*INN*) is positive for all three models and significant in the case of the production of innovations. Thus the environment of the firm, the sector in which the firm is located, is more important for non-innovating firms than the firm-specific innovation variable. For the innovating firms the innovation level of the sector in which the firm is located appears to have no positive impact on exports. In the case of sector-level R&D there is a negative and significant relationship between R&D undertaken by other firms in the sector and export performance. This may be due to rivalry between firms. While innovating firms are enjoying positive trade effects from their own R&D, they are not benefiting from the R&D undertaken by other firms in the same sector.

The capital intensity variable has no relationship with exports for the non-innovating firms, but a positive and significant one for the innovating firms. For the innovating firms the capital intensity variable alone explains 17 per cent of the variation in exports, and there is a clear positive relationship between the two. It appears that while capital intensity is a competitive asset to the innovating quoted firms, this is not the case for the non-innovating quoted firms, which have no significant relationship between exports and capital intensity. This confirms the importance of capital, as embodying innovation for the innovating firms.

There is strong evidence for the skills hypothesis for all firms, with the coefficient on the average salary variable being positive and significant in all cases. The unit labour-cost variable results are similar to the earlier results for all the firms. Unit labour costs are not significantly linked to trade performance for the innovating firms, but for the non-innovating firms they have a negative and significant relationship. This result indicates that non-innovating firms may compete more on cost than innovating firms, which are in some way insulated from cost competition through their status as innovators.

To summarize, the quoted firms were taken as a relatively homogeneous group of firms within the entire sample of firms. This choice was also motivated by the availability of firm R&D data for those firms. Clearly, this reduces the number of firms considered to less than half the sample, leaving 170 firms. Most of the firms in this sample export (with the exception of 14 firms), so the results concentrate on the propensity to export. The capital intensity variable appears to be important only for the innovating firms, while there is some evidence of the importance of firm-level skills on export performance for both groups of firms. Firm-level innovation is important in influencing the export performance of the innovating firms, while the innovation environment has more impact on the non-innovating firms. This indicates a greater role for inter-firm spillovers for the non-innovating firms, while the innovating firms' export behaviour seems to be influenced only by their own R&D.

6.7 CONCLUSIONS

This chapter has analysed the role of firm-specific characteristics in influencing trade performance at the microeconomic level. It is complementary to the other chapters, which have concentrated on sector and country characteristics as determinants of trade performance at the national and sectoral level. In addition to firm characteristics, some characteristics of the sector in which the firm is located have been included, in particular the innovation characteristics of the sector. The microeconomic data set used is unusual for two reasons: it encompasses firms of all sizes, including non-quoted firms; and the firms are divided into two groups, innovating and non-innovating firms, on the basis of their innovation history rather than their R&D expenditure. For this sample of firms some of the non-innovating firms have R&D expenditure, while some of the innovators do not, so the use of actual innovations produces a different classification from that based on R&D expenditure. This should avoid some of the biases which occur using R&D expenditure as a proxy for innovation, such as underestimating the contribution of small firms to innovation.

Considering the relationship between trade and innovation at the firm level has a number of advantages. It is only at the firm level that the balance between the relative influence of firm and sector characteristics on firm behaviour can be considered. In this analysis both sector-specific and firm-specific determinants are included, and their roles are examined. As the results show, the relative importance of sector and firm characteristics does vary with the type of firm being considered; a result which cannot be obtained at the sector level. Dividing the determinants of export behaviour into *firm*-specific characteristics and *sector*-specific characteristics, the former appear to be more important for innovating firms than for non-innovating firms, and the latter for non-innovators. This can be seen for firm-level capital intensity, which is a more important determinant of the level of exports for innovating firms, and for firm R&D expenditure.

As far as sector-specific characteristics are concerned, non-innovating firms appear to have their export behaviour influenced by domestic market size. However, this influence does not extend to innovating firms. In addition, the role of sector-level innovation, or the level of technological opportunity at the sector level, plays a much greater role in determining the export performance of non-innovating firms than of innovating firms. The R&D expenditure undertaken by firms classified as non-innovating appears to have little impact on their export performance.

Another advantage of examining trade behaviour at the firm level is the potential heterogeneity between firms. Studies at the aggregate or sectoral level abstract from variations among firms. As this firm-level study shows, there are considerable differences in the reactions of innovating and non-innovating firms, and in the determinants of their export behaviour. This implies that the capacity to innovate fundamentally changes the performance of the firm, and the determinants of exports at the firm level.

Considering the quoted firms alone, firm-level R&D expenditure and capital intensity have a positive impact on the exports of the innovating firms, confirming the importance of competitive advantage at the firm level in influencing exports. For the non-innovating firms, the production of innovations in the sector, rather than the firm's own R&D expenditure, has a positive effect on exports. Thus it appears that the firm-specific advantages of innovation are more important for the innovating firms than the innovation characteristics of the sector in which the firm is located. Past firm-specific innovations which have been incorporated into the capital of the firm, shown by capital intensity, also contribute to its present competitiveness. Thus innovation is in part cumulated at the firm level in capital stock; past and present innovations and innovation potential (R&D expenditure) have a positive impact on firm performance in international markets.

The results of the analysis confirm that innovation at the microeconomic level is a fundamental characteristic which alters the nature of the firm and its performance. It provides microeconomic evidence of the role of innovation in affecting trade performance, which has been so widely discussed at the macroeconomic level.

The implications for government policy are considerable. First, it appears that promoting innovation at the level of the firm can considerably improve export performance. In addition, the general level of innovation at the sector level can improve the trade performance of non-innovative firms, indicating that there are spillovers from innovation to the trade performance of all firms. Government policies to stimulate innovation could improve general competitiveness, by promoting the level of innovation at the sector level.

Second, in terms of the labour market, low wages appear to play no role in export performance at the firm level. In contrast, firms with higher average remuneration are both more likely to export and are more successful on export markets, reflecting the importance of skills in export performance. This is the case for both innovating and non-innovating firms. Taking into account the evidence presented in Section 2, indicating that the average level of education in the UK has negatively affected trade performance, there appears to be some scope for improvements in the skills of the workforce. As far as the results here are concerned, skills appear to be a much more important determinant of export behaviour at the firm level than low wages; therefore it is the former that should become a major objective of government policy rather than keeping down wage levels to improve competitiveness.

NOTES

1. See, for instance, Lundvall (1992), for a theoretical assessment, and Nelson (1993) and Archibugi and Pianta (1992) for detailed country-level analyses.
2. There is a well-developed empirical literature on the relationship between multinationalization and firm performance. For a recent contribution examining the impact on firm growth, see Cantwell and Sanna-Randaccio (1993).
3. See Pavitt (1984) for details of the distribution of firms according to size and innovation characteristics for this survey.
4. See Kamien and Schwartz (1982) and Dosi (1988) for more details.
5. Brech and Stout (1981) have also looked at the relationship between devaluations in the exchange rate and non-price competitiveness in the UK. They conclude that particularly in the machine tools sector, devaluations have led to a decline in product quality over time.
6. This is not a recent phenomenon: Crafts and Thomas (1986) point out that even prior to the Second World War, the UK did not appear to have a comparative advantage in human-capital-intensive goods.
7. For other studies on the UK, see Cable and Rebelo (1981), Lyons (1989) and Maskus et al. (1994) for a neo-endowment model of labour skills in UK trade.
8. For details of the data sources, see the Appendix.
9. Note that this is less than in the US data set used by Acs and Audretsch (1988) where almost half of the innovations come from firms with fewer than 500 employees.
10. Defined as being between 2700 and 4992 of the 1968 SIC classification.

11. More than 500,000 non-quoted firms with an output of more than half a million pounds a year are covered by the non-quoted data set.
12. See Cantwell (1994) for a review of the relationship between international production and trade, and the importance of innovation in influencing intra-firm trade.
13. Capital intensity is defined relative to sales and not to labour, as the capital to labour ratio was found to be collinear with the average remuneration variable, making it difficult to separate the effects of the two variables.
14. Innovations were reclassified from the 1968 SIC classification to the 1980 SIC classification following the official correspondence available from the CSO.
15. These results are the same substituting *PROD* for *USER*.
16. The relationship between the use and production of innovations between firms and sectors in the SPRU survey is complex. Pavitt (1984) has suggested a three-tier classification based partly on the use and production of innovation.
17. The R&D of each individual firm is excluded in turn from sector R&D expenditure.

APPENDIX 6A DATA SOURCES

The sector distribution of firms from the sample is given below. The two-digit 1980 revised SIC classification is in brackets. It was not possible to classify all firms, reducing the total number of firms to 496.

Table 6A.1 The sector distribution of firms

Sector	Innovators	Non-innovators
1. Metal manufacturing (22)	4	6
2. Non-metallic manufacturing (24)	6	15
3. Chemical and man-made products (25, 26)	21	18
4. Other metal goods (31)	5	23
5. Mechanical engineering (32)	60	51
6. Office and data machinery (33)	18	5
7. Electrical and electronic machinery (34)	29	38
8. Motor vehicles and parts (35)	5	5
9. Other transport (36)	13	5
10. Instrument engineering (37)	23	6
11. Food, drink and tobacco (41, 42)	7	21
12. Textiles (43)	–	13
13. Leather goods (44)	–	–
14. Footwear and clothing (45)	1	11
15. Timber (46)	6	14
16. Paper and printing (47)	6	18
17. Rubber and plastics (48)	6	18
18. Other manufacturing (49)	4	15
Total	214	282

Data on innovations come from 'Innovation in the UK since 1945', Science Policy Research Unit, University of Sussex, from the ESRC archive, Essex.

Additional firm balance sheet data: total sales, exports, total capital, average remuneration, the number of employees came from two sources – Datastream for the quoted firms (including firm-level R&D expenditure), and ICC for the non-quoted firms.

The sector-level data: total UK manufacturing output and sector output came from the Central Statistical Office, *Report on the Census of Production*, 1991 Summary Volume, PA 1002.

The sector-level R&D expenditure from First Release, CSO No. 188, December 1993, 'Business Enterprise Research and Development 1992'.

PART IV

Conclusions

7. Conclusions and Policy Implications

The main objective of this book has been to evaluate the importance of innovation in influencing the trade performance of industrialized countries. Two different perspectives are taken in this evaluation: a macroeconomic perspective and a firm-level analysis. The former considers the relationship between differences in bilateral trade performance and innovation across a number of sectors, and for each sector across different bilateral flows. Differences in innovation are assumed to be a major determinant of net trade performance between industrialized countries. The influence of sector and country characteristics on the relationship between trade and innovation is particularly highlighted. This sector-level perspective abstracts from individual firms, and considers the aggregate behaviour of firms operating within certain sectors and countries. Using the country and the sector as the level of analysis reflects the technological characteristics which are peculiar to certain countries and certain sectors.

In the second part of the book, the firm is taken as the unit of analysis; this approach abstracts from some aspects of technology that are exogenous to the individual firm. These include the structure of the economy, the inter-linkages between different sectors in the economy, and the institutions of the economy, which can be broadly termed the national system of innovation; none of these can in general be influenced by an individual firm. As all the firms considered are in the UK, it is not possible to analyse the impact of different national characteristics on the export behaviour of the firms. The microeconomic analysis does not therefore aim to explain national and sectoral differences in innovation, and the impact they have on international trade. Rather, the aim is to consider the innovation undertaken by individual firms and the impact this has both on their competitiveness in international markets, and on the probability of them entering those export markets. The impact of the characteristics of the sector in which the firm is located are also considered in the analysis as well as the interaction between sector and firm characteristics.

Part I presents the theoretical background and reviews the empirical work relating technology to trade. The theoretical framework for this study is the technology gap model, and the subsequent extensions to it taking into account additional features of innovation as well as monopoly power. As a result of these extensions, the temporary advantage hypothesized by the technology gap model, in which the diffusion of technology to other countries occurs automatically, is balanced by a view of technology which stresses the cumulative and path-dependent nature of technological change. The main assumption behind the choice of framework is that 'knowledge', of which innovation forms a part, is taken to be the most *important* resource in the modern economy. For international trade this means that differences in innovation provide the basis for specialization and trade between countries. Thus international competitiveness is based on a country's knowledge base, which is built up both through the process of learning and through innovation.

The underlying view of innovation assumed in this study is outlined at the beginning of Chapter 6. Innovation is characterized as a cumulative process: past experience in innovation affects present innovation, leading to path dependency at the level both of the individual firm and of the country. The process of innovation at the level of the firm is seen as a *search* process, in which firms are constrained by their present knowledge and capabilities. Present production techniques and limitations form the basic agenda upon which the search is based, so that search is *local*. Innovation is also surrounded by uncertainty, due to both the uncertainty of science, that is, what is technically possible, and the uncertainty associated with the economic significance of innovations.

Innovation is thus a process which is difficult to date precisely; the traditional classification of the process into the three phases of invention, innovation and diffusion may be hard to observe in practice. In dividing firms into innovating and non-innovating firms based on their innovation history (from 1945 to 1983) in Part III, the capacity to innovate is viewed as a long-term phenomenon which fundamentally changes the nature of the firm. The separation of firms into innovating and non-innovating firms is consistent with the characterization of technology as firm specific and cumulative. The differences between the two groups of firms are confirmed both by descriptive statistics, and by the econometric analysis. Innovation gives a specific competitive advantage to a firm which, because of the cumulative nature of technological development, can remain firm specific over time. This is reflected in the different firm characteristics shown by the innovating and non-innovating firms in terms of, for instance, firm size. The determinants of export performance also appear to vary according to the innovation characteristics of the firm.

The same view of innovation underlies the earlier sector-level analysis of Part II. Innovation is considered to be at least partly appropriable, so part of the benefits remain localized within the innovating sector and country, giving them a competitive advantage on international markets. Technology does not automatically diffuse over national boundaries, even within sectors, and thus a particular sector in a country may have a superior technology to that sector in other countries, providing the basis for international trade. In addition to the actions of individual firms, the sector-level analysis can also take account of the national and sectoral dimensions of innovation, which are more than the sum of the actions of individual firms. The structural links of the economy, and the spillovers of innovation domestically between sectors, all influence national and sectoral innovation patterns. By allowing the relationship to vary according to the sector and country concerned, particular attention is given in Part II to the importance of common sector and national characteristics in influencing trade. The national characteristics reflect the common conditions within the country, such as institutions and domestic industrial structure. The characteristics of the sector include, for instance, the level of technological opportunity in the sector, and demand conditions in the sector.

Part II starts with an analysis of the correlations between differences in innovation, proxied by two different patent indicators, and bilateral trade performance between four European countries. The relationship was considered for 40 sectors, varying from very-high-technology sectors such as aerospace, to resource-based sectors such as petroleum. Four European countries were chosen as they represent similar and highly integrated countries, among which the diffusion of technology should be relatively straightforward. These countries are integrated in a number of ways, through trade, as they are important mutual trading partners, and foreign direct investment through MNCs, as well as co-operative agreements between firms and joint ventures. They are also undergoing a process of both economic and political integration, including a European-level science and technology policy. As a result, the European countries, and in particular the four studied in Chapter 4, have a number of features supporting the diffusion of technology between them. The existence of technology gaps between these countries therefore confirms the view that technology can remain specific to a sector and country, in spite of greater integration.

The results indicate that on a country level both Germany and France have their bilateral flows positively related to differences in innovation. When the export market shares of each of the four European countries in the forty sectors are related to their share of innovation in each sector, positive relationships between the two are found for all four countries; in the case of the UK, this occurs only when the two sectors of armaments and petroleum are removed from the study. These two sectors make up an important part of the UK innovation profile, and trade in them does not appear to be influenced by technology when proxied by patents. In general, however, the trade of the

UK with the other three countries, and more generally in Europe, is influenced by innovation, with the exception of these two important sectors.

For the sector-level results, twenty out of forty sectors appear to be positively and significantly influenced by differences in bilateral innovation. With the exception of one sector (textile products), all the sectors showing a significant correlation between differences in innovation and trade are medium-technology or high-technology sectors. However, this is not the case for all the high-technology sectors; trade in some does not appear to be influenced by either relative patenting or relative R&D expenditure. This reflects the difficulty of capturing the role of innovation, particularly in sectors which are experiencing a fast pace of technological change. In general, the results indicate two points. First, that differences in technology are an important determinant of trade performance between the European countries; for eight of the sectors differences in technology alone could explain 50 per cent or more of bilateral trade performance. Second, the relationship appears to vary substantially over sectors, and according to which bilateral flow is considered. This result confirms that there are a number of determinants of trade and no one factor in isolation can explain all intra-European trade flows. Nevertheless, while not being the *only* determinant of trade, differences in innovation are a significant determinant of trade between the European countries.

In response to the necessity of including additional factors in determining trade performance, Chapter 5 estimates a more complete model of trade performance, and also includes a larger sample of countries. As well as considering differences in innovation proxied both by R&D expenditure and patents, the model includes differences in labour costs between countries in each sector (in this chapter, 22 manufacturing sectors are taken), and differences in investment rates. As in Chapter 4, the data are both sector and country specific, allowing differences across countries to be examined. Initially dummy variables were included for the country, the sector, and both country and sector together. Country dummies are found to be highly significant, while those for the sectors are not. These country effects reflect the importance of omitted variables which vary from country to country, such as the institutions of that country, the exchange rate regime, domestic demand conditions, and other influences which are specific to each country and affect all the trade flows from that country.

Although dummy variables allow the relationship to vary to some extent, the impact of the explanatory variables may also vary by sector and by country; the unrestricted models allowing variations by country or by sector are also tested relative to the restricted pooling. In the case of the country, the restriction of pooling is rejected at 5 per cent but not at 1 per cent, and for the sectors it is rejected at 1 per cent, indicating that the determinants of trade performance vary considerably according to the country, but above all with the sector. Taking the sector results, all three of the explanatory variables matched *a priori* expectations in at least half of the sectors. Both the investment and the innovation variable are expected to be positively related to trade performance. Indeed, investment is considered to be complementary to innovation, as many new innovations are embodied in capital machinery which requires investment. For the labour-cost variable, a negative relationship is expected, as low labour costs should give a cost advantage in export markets. Considering both the model using the R&D-based technology variable, and that using the patent-based variable, 16 of the 22 sectors have positive and significant relationships between trade performance and innovation, using one or other of the proxies. This is more than for either of the other two variables, for which eleven sectors show significant relationships that are consistent with *a priori* expectations. These results therefore confirm the importance of differences in innovation as a determinant of bilateral trade performance, when including additional explanatory variables. Once again the majority of the sectors for which the relationship is significant is made up of high-technology and medium-technology industries.

Finally, in Chapter 5 a separate model was estimated for the UK using actual counts of innovation as an alternative to the innovation proxies. As the innovation counts were available only for the UK, only the trade flows including the UK were used. In addition, the model was estimated with gross exports as the dependent variable, as the innovation variables reflect only domestic innovation rather than differences in innovation between countries. The results showed that both innovations *produced* in a sector, and innovations *used* in that sector have a positive impact on gross exports. This confirms the role of innovation in trade, which was established using the proxies for innovation. It also indicates that innovations benefit both the sectors which produce them and those sectors which subsequently use the innovations.

As the counts of innovation are available on a sector basis and include both innovations used in each sector and innovations produced, the ratio between the two can be used to classify sectors either into net users or net producers of innovations. The survey from which the innovation data are taken shows that in the majority of cases innovations are used in sectors other than the one in which they originate. This indicates that domestic spillovers between sectors are very important. On examination, there are a number of sectors (such as the machinery sectors) which are important producers of innovations subsequently used in other sectors. In order to consider the difference between sectors which use and produce sectors, the 22 sectors of the analysis are split into net users and net producers, and the model for the determinants of trade performance is reestimated for the two groups. The clearest result is that technology, proxied by R&D expenditure, has a positive impact on trade performance for the producing sectors, but not for the using sectors. The latter may not rely on their own R&D expenditure, but rather free ride on the benefits of the R&D expenditure of the innovating sectors. In addition, R&D expenditure does not reveal the full impact of innovation in the net using sectors, as innovations originating in other sectors will not be reflected in the using sector's R&D expenditure, although they nevertheless have an impact on performance in the sector.

Overall, the two chapters in Part II show the importance of differences in innovation in affecting bilateral trade performance between developed countries. Differences in technology are a significant determinant of trade performance in more sectors than either relative labour costs or relative investment when considering nine OECD countries. For the four European countries in Chapter 4, each country's share of innovation positively and significantly affects its share of exports in Europe. While the results confirm the importance of technology, they also indicate that its significance as a determinant of trade varies both with the countries being considered, and in particular with the sector. For some sectors, noticeably low-technology sectors, differences in innovation play only a small role in trade performance, which appears to be dominated by relative cost considerations. This is consistent with other results considering the relationship between trade and technology. The extension of the analysis in Chapter 5, using actual innovations divided into innovations produced and used, also indicates the impact of innovation on gross exports for the UK.

The results confirm the existence of technology gaps between advanced countries, both within Europe and between OECD countries. This is contradictory to the idea that with increased trade and integration, and the globalization of production, technology gaps among countries cannot survive. The evidence from these sector-level studies is that in the late 1980s technology gaps remain between similar and highly developed countries with close trade links and even, in the case of the European countries, political and institutional links, and are an important determinant of bilateral trade performance between them.

In Part III, the unit of analysis changes from the sector to the firm, in order to consider the role of innovation at the microeconomic level. The firms included in the sample are both quoted and non-quoted firms, and cover the spectrum of firm sizes. The innovating firms were chosen from the innovation survey undertaken by SPRU, while the non-innovators were chosen randomly. The classification into innovators and non-innovators is thus based on a firm's inclusion or exclusion from the survey, which is assumed to provide a more reliable indicator of a firm's innovation history than R&D expenditure would; in particular it should not suffer from the size bias often noted with using R&D expenditure as an indicator of innovation.

The results support the separation of firms into innovating and non-innovating firms, rather than grouping them together. This confirms the notion that innovation fundamentally changes the firm and that the determinants of export behaviour vary over the two groups of firms. In particular, dividing the determinants of trade into firm-specific and sector-specific characteristics, it is the former rather than the latter which appear to influence the trade performance of the innovating firms. The significant firm characteristics are capital intensity, average wages and firm size, all of which are positively related to exports for the innovating firms. With the exception of the capital intensity variable, these variables are also positively related to exports for the non-innovating firms. As far as the sector characteristics are concerned, the size of the domestic market and the sector level of innovation affect the non-innovating firms' export behaviour, in particular the probability of them exporting, but have no effect on that of the innovating firms. We can conclude that it is characteristics specific to the firm which are more important for the innovating firms, while the non-innovating firms are also influenced by the characteristics of the sector in which they are located.

As far as R&D expenditure is concerned, firm-level R&D expenditure has a positive and significant impact on the exports of the innovating firms, but it is sector-level R&D expenditure, rather than firm level, which positively affects the non-innovating firms. These results confirm the results of Part II: innovation has a positive impact on trade performance at the firm level, as well as at the sector level between countries. In particular, the role of technology changes according to the innovation characteristics of the firm being considered, for innovating firms, their own innovations and their commitment of resources to research have a positive impact on their trade performance. For firms classified as non-innovators, the innovation level of the sector in which they are located has a positive impact on their trade performance, although their in-house commitment to research does not appear to significantly influence their trade performance.

Overall, the results confirm the importance of innovation as a determinant of trade performance at the level of the country, the sector and the firm. This supports the notion that innovation is one of the most important resources in the modern economy, which is reflected in the role of differences in innovation in influencing international competitiveness.

There is one serious drawback to treating trade performance as the only indicator of the international competitiveness of a country. One feature of the international economic order is that a large and growing part of the post-war increase in international trade has been intra-firm trade between subsidiaries of multinational companies, reflecting the increasing globalization of production, and the rising importance of foreign direct investment as part of international transactions. Thus, when taking international trade as an indication of the competitiveness of an economy, one important element – that of foreign direct investment – is missing. The direct investment overseas of MNCs reflects the competitiveness of domestic firms on the international market, and is not captured by exports. As a result, concentrating on the trade performance of a country ignores the performance of that country's MNCs abroad.

Innovation, and in particular the firm-specific competitive advantage that results from innovation, is considered a strong motivation for direct investment overseas in place of exports, or other arm's-length transactions (Cantwell, 1989; Narula, 1995). Thus it may be particularly in the case of firm-specific technological advantages that overseas production takes precedence over exports. Nevertheless, as the analysis in Chapter 6 shows, firm-specific technological advantages also have a positive effect on the export performance of firms. So the firm-specific benefits of innovation can influence *export* behaviour as well as acting as an incentive for the internalization of production. The role of innovation in promoting foreign production is an avenue for future research.

Another limitation that is associated with econometric studies is that in quantifying a process as complex as technological change, inevitably some simplification is required. In particular, capturing the interrelationships between innovation in different sectors is problematic. Both the patent and R&D expenditure variables used in Chapters 4 and 5 are calculated for a particular sector, and do not take account of the influence of innovations from other sectors. Including the actual innovation data taken from the survey, which notes both the sector in which the innovation is produced and that in which it is used, partly deals with this problem; the impact of the innovations on the using and the producing sectors can be analysed. The significant relationship found between gross exports and innovations used in the sector shows that the use as well as the production of innovation positively affects trade performance. As the use of innovations is not necessarily captured by either R&D expenditure or patents they may underestimate the importance of innovation in some sectors which, while not producing many innovations, are influenced by innovations originating in other sectors. However, the innovation data are only for the UK and are therefore absolute rather than relative to other countries, for an international analysis the innovation proxies used have the advantage of being across countries rather than for a single country.

The importance of differences in innovation in influencing international competitiveness is of particular interest to governments and international agencies because of the key role that technology plays in economic growth. National governments are increasingly concerned with targeting certain industries, and in particular high-technology industries, in a strategic attempt to improve exports and economic growth, often based on the example of MITI in influencing Japan's economic growth. National governments wish to have high-technology sectors located in their own countries, because of the high valued added and high growth characteristics of these sectors. As a result, science and technology policy has become increasingly linked to trade policy in many industrialized countries, with trade negotiations also touching on issues traditionally of interest only to technology policy makers.[1] However, the results of this study indicate that innovation does not just affect high-technology industries, but it is also a key determinant of trade performance in a number of medium-technology industries, in particular in the machinery sectors. Thus the potential impact of domestic technology policy can be broader than just high-technology industries. In addition, innovations produced in one sector can affect the performance of sectors which use those innovations, although the innovation-producing sector's performance does not necessarily suffer as a result. Rather, the results presented in Chapter 5 indicate that both the producing and the using sectors benefit from the innovations. The implication for technology policy is that promoting innovation can have an amplified impact on the economy, as it benefits both the sector which innovates and the sector in which the innovation is applied.

In general, the results indicate that firms do benefit from their innovations, and that although the benefits of innovation may be only *partly* appropriable, they do appear to give a competitive advantage to the firm. Innovating firms are generally larger, more likely to export, and export a higher proportion of their output. Countries which innovate more than their trading partners also appear to benefit from the innovation through improved trade performance and a higher share of the export market. This is reassuring to technology policy makers, who may consider that with internationalization, and increased integration, the benefits of domestic innovation can be exploited by foreign competitors, and that as a result subsidizing domestic innovation also acts as a subsidy to those competitors. Rather, the results presented earlier indicate that the benefits of innovation accrue at least partly to the innovator, whether it is at the level of the individual firm or the level of the country.

Partly as a result of innovation benefiting the innovating countries, technology gaps appear to exist among the OECD countries. Given the implications that technology gaps have for economic growth (Verspagen, 1993; Fagerberg, 1988), this can have serious consequences for economic convergence. In the context of the process of European union, the results indicate that in addition to the financial criteria included in the Maastricht Treaty, differences in innovation should also be considered as they present an important source of divergence between the European countries. The basis of this evidence is not trade between the less- and more-developed countries in the EU, but rather trade between four of the most advanced countries in Europe – France, Germany, the UK and the Netherlands. That technology gaps exist between these countries indicates that countries at a similar level of development can also have different levels and patterns of innovation. As far as technology policy at the European level is concerned, it is not just the transfer of knowledge and competences from the advanced to the less-advanced countries in Europe that are important, but also variations in the commitment or resources to innovation by all the European countries which deserve attention.

Finally, for domestic policy the results indicate that differences in innovation are more important in influencing competitiveness than differences in labour costs, although the latter do play a role in some sectors. The debate about competitiveness often focuses solely on differences in labour costs, and stresses the need to keep labour costs down in order to remain competitive. This would appear to be an effective way to improve competitiveness in some sectors, but improvements to domestic innovation rates have a positive effect on trade performance in a greater number of sectors, and especially in those sectors often considered to be desirable by national governments. As far as the impact of labour costs is concerned, the evidence appears to be contradictory. Labour costs were found to be negatively related to net trade, but positively to gross trade in the case of the UK, indicating that high wages have a positive effect on UK exports, although the net trade balance is negatively affected by them. At the level of the individual firm, exports were positively related to the average salary of the firm, for both innovating and non-innovating firms; and unit labour costs were also positively related to trade performance for the innovating firms. This is taken as support for the positive effect of skills on export performance, assuming that higher wages reflect a higher skill composition of the firm's labour force. Overall, the importance of innovation, and the positive role of skills in determining trade performance, indicate that international competitiveness does not have to be based on low labour costs, particularly in the context of trade between developed countries, but instead a competitive advantage can be created through innovation and improving the education of the workforce.

NOTE

1. See Mowery (1992), for a discussion of the challenge of trade to technology policy, and Yoffie (1992) for the challenge of technology to trade policy.

References

Abd-el-Rahman, K. (1991), 'Firms' Competitive and National Comparative Advantages as Joint Determinants of Trade Composition', *Weltwirtschaftliches Archiv*, **127** (1), pp. 83–98.

Abromovitz, M.A. (1986), 'Catching Up, Forging Ahead and Falling Behind', *Journal of Economic History*, **46**, pp. 385–406.

Acs, Z.J. and D.B. Audretsch (1988), 'Innovation in Large and Small Firms: An Empirical Analysis', *American Economic Review*, **78** (4), pp. 678–90.

Acs, Z.J. and D.B. Audretsch (1989), 'Patents as a Measure of Innovative Activity', *Kyklos*, **42** (2), pp. 171–80.

Aharoni, Y. and S. Hirsch (1993), 'Enhancing the Competitive Advantage of Developing Countries in Technology-Intensive Industries: A Conceptual Scheme and Policy Implications', *Working Paper 1–93*, Institute of International Economics and Management, Copenhagen Business School.

Amable, B. and B. Verspagen (1995), 'The Role of Technology in Market Share Dynamics', *Applied Economics*, **27**, pp. 197–204.

Amendola, G., G. Dosi and E. Papagni (1993), 'The Dynamic of International Competitiveness', *Weltwirtschaftliches Archiv*, **129** (3), pp. 451–71.

Amendola, G., P. Guerrieri, and P. Padoan (1991), 'International Patterns of Technological Accumulation and Trade', *CIDEI Working Paper* No. 3, 'La Sapienza', Rome.

Anderton, R. (1992), 'UK Exports of Manufactures: Testing for the Effects of Non-price Competitiveness using Stochastic Trends and Profitability Measures', *The Manchester School*, **LX** (1), pp. 23–40.

Antonelli, C. (1986), 'The International Diffusion of Process Innovations and the Neotechnology Theory of International Trade', *Economic Notes*, **1**, pp. 60–83.

Aquino, A. (1981), 'Changes Over Time in the Pattern of Comparative Advantage in Manufactured Goods', *European Economic Review*, **15**, pp. 41–62.

Archibugi, D. and M. Pianta (1992), *The Technological Specialization of Advanced Countries: A Report to the EEC on International Science and Technology Activities*, Boston: Kluwer Academic Publishers.

Archibugi, D. and M. Pianta (1993), 'Patterns of Technological Specialisation and Growth of Innovative Activities in Advanced Countries', in K. Hughes (ed.), *European Competitiveness*, Cambridge: Cambridge University Press, pp. 105–32.

Arthur, W.B. (1989), 'Competing Technologies, Increasing Returns and Lock-in by Historical Events', *Economic Journal*, **99**, pp. 116–31.

Audretsch, D.B. (1987), 'An Empirical Test of the Industry Life Cycle', *Weltwirtschaftliches Archiv*, **123** (2), pp. 297–308.

Audretsch, D.B. and H. Yamawaki (1987), 'R&D Rivalry, Industrial Policy and US–Japanese Trade', *Review of Economics and Statistics*, **69**, pp. 438–47.

Balassa, B. (1965), 'Trade Liberalization and "Revealed Comparative Advantage"', *The Manchester School of Economic and Social Studies*, **33**, pp. 99–123.

Balassa, B. (1986), 'The Determinants of Intra-Industry Specialisation in United States Trade', *Oxford Economic Papers*, **38**, pp. 220–33.

Balassa, B. and L. Bauwens (1987), 'Intra-industry Specialisation in a Multi-country and Multi-industry Framework', *Economic Journal*, **97**, pp. 923–39.

Balassa, B. and L. Bauwens (1988), 'The Determinants of Intra-European Trade in Manufactured Goods', *European Economic Review*, **32**, pp. 1421–37.

Baldwin, R. (1971), 'Determinants of the Commodity Structure of US Trade', *American Economic Review*, **61**, pp. 126–46.

Basberg, B. (1982), 'Technological Change in the Norwegian Whaling Industry: A Case Study of the Use of Patent Statistics as a Technology Indicator, *Research Policy*, **11** (3), pp. 163–71.

Basberg, B. (1983), 'Foreign Patenting in the USA as a Technology Indicator: The Case of Norway', *Research Policy*, **12**, pp. 227–37.

Basberg, B. (1987), 'Patents and the Measurement of Technological Change: A Survey of the Literature', *Research Policy*, **16**, pp. 131–41.

Baumol, W.J. (1986), 'Productivity Growth, Convergence and Welfare: What the Long Run Data Show', *American Economic Review*, **76** (5), pp. 1072–85.

Baumol, W.J., S.A. Blackman and E.N. Wolff (1989), '*Productivity and American Leadership*', Cambridge, MA: MIT Press.

Bensel, T. and B.T. Elmslie (1992), 'Rethinking International Trade Theory: A Methodological Appraisal', *Weltwirtshaftliches Archiv*, **128**, pp. 249–65.

Bergstrand, J.H. (1990), 'The Heckscher–Ohlin–Samuelson Model, the Linder Hypothesis and the Determinants of Bilateral Intra-industry Trade', *Economic Journal*, **100**, pp. 1216–29.

Blomstrom, M., R. Lipsey and L. Ohlsson (1990), 'What do Rich Countries Trade With Each Other? R&D and the Composition of US/Swedish Trade', *Banco Nazionale del Lavoro Quarterly Review*, **173**, pp. 215–35.

Bonaccorsi, A. (1992), 'On the Relationship between Firm Size and Export Intensity', *Journal of International Business Studies*, **23** (4), pp. 605–35.

Bowen, H. (1980), 'Resources, Technology and Dynamic Comparative Advantage: A Cross-Section Analysis of the Product Cycle Theory of International Trade', Unpublished PhD dissertation, mimeo.

Bowen, H., E.E. Leamer and L.Sveikaukas (1987), 'Multicountry, Multifactor Tests of the Factor Abundance Theory', *American Economic Review*, **77**, pp. 791–809.

Brander, J. and B. Spencer (1983), 'International R&D Rivalry and Industrial Strategy', *Review of Economic Studies*, **50** (4), pp. 707–22.

Brech, M.J. and D.K. Stout (1981), 'The Rate of Exchange and Non-price Competitiveness: A Provisional Study within UK Manufacturing Exports', *Oxford Economic Papers*, **33** Supplement, pp. 268–81.

Buxton, T., D. Mayes and A. Murfin (1991), 'UK Trade Performance and R&D', *Economics of Innovation and New Technology*, **1**, pp. 243–56.

Cable, V. and I. Rebelo (1981), 'Britain's Pattern of Specialisation in Manufactured Goods with Developing Countries and Trade Protection', *World Bank Staff Working Paper*, No. 425.

Cantwell, J. (1989), *Technological Innovation and Multinational Corporations*, Oxford: Basil Blackwell.

Cantwell, J. (1994), 'The Relationship between International Trade and International Production', in D. Greenaway and L. Alan Winters (eds), *Surveys in International Trade*, Oxford: Basil Blackwell, pp. 303–28.

Cantwell, J. and F. Sanna-Randaccio (1993), 'Multinationality and Firm Growth', *Weltwirtshaftliches Archiv*, **129**, pp. 275–99.

Caves, R. (1981), 'Intra-industry Trade and Market Structure in the Industrialised Countries', *Oxford Economic Papers*, **33**, pp. 203–23.

Chesnais, F. (1986), 'Science, Technology and Competitiveness', *Science, Technology and Industry Review*, **1**, pp. 85–129.

Chesnais, F. (1992), 'National Systems of Innovation, Foreign Direct Investment and the Operations of Multinational Enterprises', in B.A. Lundvall (ed.), *National Systems of Innovation*, London: Pinter, pp. 265–95.

Cimoli, M. (1988), 'Technological Gaps and Institutional Asymmetries in a North–South Model with a Continuum of Goods', *Metroeconomica*, **39**, pp. 245–74.

Cotsomitis, J., C. De Bresson, and A. Kwan (1991), 'A Re-examination of the Technology Gap Theory of Trade: Some Evidence from Time Series Data for OECD Countries', *Weltwirtshaftliches Archiv*, **127**, pp. 792–9.

Courakis, A.S. (1991), 'Labour Skills and Human Capital in the Explanation of Trade Patterns', *Oxford Economic Papers*, **43**, pp. 443–62.

Crafts, N.F.R. and M. Thomas (1986), 'Comparative Advantage in UK Manufacturing Trade', 1910–1935', *Economic Journal*, **96**, pp. 629–45.

Cragg, J. (1971), 'Some Statistical Models for Limited Dependent Variables with Application to the Demand for Durable Goods', *Econometrica*, **39**, pp. 829–44.

Dalum, B. (1992), 'Export Specialisation, Structural Competitiveness and National Systems of Innovation', in B.A. Lundvall (ed.), *National Systems of Innovation*, London: Pinter, pp. 191–225.

Daniels, P. (1993), 'Research and Development, Human Capital and Trade Performance in Technology Intensive Manufactures: A Cross-country Analysis', *Research Policy*, **22**, pp. 207–41.

David, P.A. (1975), *Technological Change, Innovation and Economic Growth*, Cambridge: Cambridge University Press.

David, P.A. (1990), 'The Dynamo and the Computer: An Historical Perspective on the Modern Productivity Paradox', *American Economic Review Papers and Proceedings*, **80**, pp. 355–61.

Davidson, R. and J. MacKinnon (1981), 'Several Tests for Model Specification in the Presence of Multiple Alternatives', *Econometrica*, **49**, pp. 781–93.

Deardorff, A.V. (1984), 'Testing Trade Theories and Predicting Trade Flows', in R.W. Jones and P.B. Kenen, *Handbook of International Economics*, Vol. 1, Amsterdam: North-Holland, pp. 467–517.

Deardorff, A.V. (1994), 'Exploring the Limits of Comparative Advantage', *Weltwirtschaftliches Archiv*, **130** (1), pp. 1–19.

Dosi, G. (1984), *Technical Change and Industrial Transformation*, London: Macmillan.

Dosi, G. (1988), 'Sources, Procedures and Microeconomic Effects of Innovation', *Journal of Economic Literature*, **XXVI**, pp. 1120–71.

Dosi, G. and F. Chiaromonte (1990), 'The Microfoundations of Technological Change and International Trade', Paper presented at the OECD Conference on Technology and Competitiveness, June.

Dosi, G., C. Freeman, R. Nelson, G. Silverberg, and L. Soete (1988), *Technical Change and Economic Theory*, London: Pinter.

Dosi, G., K. Pavitt and L. Soete (1990), *The Economics of Technical Change and International Trade*, Brighton: Harvester Wheatsheaf.

Dosi, G. and L. Soete (1983), 'Technology Gaps and Cost-based Adjustments: Some Explorations on the Determinants of International Competitiveness', *Metroeconomica*, **12** (3), pp. 357–82.

Dunning, J. (1981), *International Production and the Multinational Enterprise*, London: George Allen & Unwin.

Dunning, J. (1993), *Multinational Enterprises and the Global Economy*, Wokingham: Addison-Wesley.

Engelsman, E. and A. van Raan (1990), *The Netherlands in Modern Technology: A Patent Based Assessment*, The Hague: Ministry of Economic Affairs.

Fagerberg, J. (1987), 'A Technology Gap Approach to Why Growth Rates Differ', *Research Policy*, **16**, pp. 87–99.

Fagerberg, J. (1988), 'International Competitiveness', *Economic Journal*, **98**, pp. 355–74.

Fagerberg, J. (1992), 'The Home Market Hypothesis Reexamined: The Impact of Domestic User–Producer Interaction on Export Specialisation', in B.A. Lundvall (ed.), *National Sytems of Innovation*, London: Pinter, pp. 226–41.

Fagerberg, J. (1994a), 'Technology and International Differences in Growth Rates', *Journal of Economic Literature*, **XXXII**, pp. 1147–75.

Fagerberg, J. (1994b), 'Is there a small Country Disadvantage in High Tech?', Paper presented at the Schumpeter Society Conference, Munster, August.

Freeman, C. (1963), 'The Plastics Industry: A Comparative Study of Research and Innovation', *National Institute Economic Review*, No. 26, pp. 22–40.

Freeman, C. (1982), *The Economics of Industrial Innovation*, 2nd edn, London: Pinter.

Freeman, C., M. Sharp and W. Walker (1991), *Technology and the Future of Europe*, London: Pinter.

Geroski, P. and S. Machin (1993), 'Innovation, Profitability and Growth over the Business Cycle', *Empirica*, **20**, pp. 35–50.

Glejser, H., A. Jacquemin, and J. Petit (1980), 'Exports in an Imperfect Competition Framework: An Analysis of 1,446 Exporters', *Quarterly Journal of Economics*, **94**, pp. 507–24.

Gomulka, S. (1990), *The Theory of Technological Change and Economic Growth*, London: Routledge.

Greenaway, D. (1983), 'The Measurement of Produce Differentiation in Empirical Studies of Trade Flows', in H. Kierzkowski (ed.), *Monopolistic Competition and International Trade*, Oxford: Oxford University Press, pp. 230–49.

Greenaway, D. and C. Milner (1984), 'A Cross-section Analysis of Intra-industry Trade in the UK', *European Economic Review*, **25**, pp. 319–44.

Greene, W. (1993), *Econometric Analysis*, 2nd edn, London: Macmillan.

Greenhalgh, C. (1990), 'Innovation and Trade Performance in the UK', *Economic Journal*, **100**, pp. 105–18.

Greenhalgh, C., B. Suer, and P. Taylor (1992), 'Trade Performance and Innovatory Activity: A Review', in C. Milner and N. Snowdon (eds), *External Imbalances and Policy Constraints in the 1990s*, London: Pinter, pp. 91–123.

Greenhalgh, C., P. Taylor and R. Wilson (1994), 'Innovation and Export Volumes and Prices, a Disaggregated Study', *Oxford Economic Papers*, **46**, pp. 102–34.

Griliches, Z. (1990), 'Patent Statistics as Economic Indicators: A Survey', *Journal of Economic Literature*, **28** (4), pp. 1661–797.

Grossman, G. and E. Helpman (1990), 'Trade, Innovation and Growth', *American Economic Review Papers and Proceedings*, **80** (2), pp. 86–91.

Grossman, G. and E. Helpman (1991), *Innovation and Growth, Technological Competition in the Global Economy*, Cambridge, MA: MIT Press.

Grubel, H. and P. Lloyd (1975), *Intra-industry Trade: The Theory and Measurement of International Trade in Different Products*, London Macmillan.

Gruber, W., D. Mehta and R. Vernon (1967), 'The R&D Factor in International Trade and International Investment of US Industries', *Journal of Political Economy*, **LXXV**, pp. 20–37.

Gruber, W. and R. Vernon (1970), 'The Technology Factor in a World Trade Matrix', in R. Vernon (ed.), *The Technology Factor in International Trade*, New York: Columbia University Press, pp. 233–72.

Grupp, H. (1991), 'Innovation Dynamics in OECD Countries: Towards a Correlated Network of R&D Intensity, Trade, Patent and Technometric Indicators', in OECD, *Technology and Productivity: The Challenge for Economic Policy*, Paris: OECD.

Guerrieri, P. (1991), 'Technology and International Trade Performance in the Most Advanced Countries', *Berkeley Working Paper*, No. 49.

Harkness, J. and J. Kyle (1975), 'Factors Influencing United States Comparative Advantage', *Journal of International Economics*, **5**, pp. 153–65.

Helpman, E. (1981), 'International Trade in the Presence of Product Differentiation, Economies of Scale and Monopolistic Competition: A Chamberlain–Heckscher–Ohlin Approach', *Journal of International Economics*, **11**, pp. 305–40.

Henderson, R., A.B. Jaffe and M. Trajtenberg (1992), 'Ivory Tower versus Corporate Laboratory: An Empirical Study of Basic Research and Appropriability', *NBER Working Paper*, No. 4146.

Hirsch, S. (1965), 'The US Electronics Industry in International Trade, *National Institute Economic Review*, No. 34, pp. 92–107.

Hirsch, S and I. Bijaoui (1985), 'R&D Intensity and Export Performance: A Micro View', *Weltwirtschaftliches Archiv*, **121**, pp. 138–51.

Hsiao, C. (1986), *Analysis of Panel Data*, Cambridge: Cambridge Univeristy Press.

Hufbauer, G. (1970), 'The Impact of National Characteristics and Technology on the Commodity Composition of Trade in Manufactured Goods', in R. Vernon (ed.), *The Technology Factor in International Trade*, New York: Columbia Universtiy Press, pp. 145–231.

Hughes, K. (1986), *Exports and Technology*, Cambridge: Cambridge University Press.

Johnson, H. (1975), 'Technological Change and Comparative Advantage: An Advanced Country's Viewpoint', *Journal of World Trade Law*, **9**, pp. 1–14.

Kaldor, N. (1978), 'The Effect of Devaluations On Trade in Manufactures', in *Further Essays on Applied Economics*, London: Duckworth.

Kaldor, M., M. Sharp and W. Walker (1986), 'Industrial Competitiveness and Britain's Defence', *Lloyds Bank Review*, No. 162, pp. 31–49.

Kamien, M. and N. Schwartz (1982), *Market Structure and Innovation*, Cambridge: Cambridge University Press.

Katrak, H. (1982), 'Labour Skills, R&D and Capital Requirements in the International Trade and Investment of the United Kingdom 1968–78', *National Institute Economic Review*, No. 101, pp. 38–47.

Kay, N. (1982), *The Evolving Firm*, London: Macmillan.

Keesing, D. (1967), 'The Impact of Research and Development on United States Trade', *Journal of Political Economy*, **75**, pp. 38–45.

Kitti, C. and D. Schiffel (1978), 'Rates of Invention: International Patent Comparisons', *Research Policy*, **7**, pp. 324–40.

Krugman, P. (1979), 'A Model of Innovation, Technology Transfer and the World Distribution of Income', *Journal of Political Economy*, **87**, pp. 253–66.

Krugman, P. (1981), 'Intraindustry Specialisation and the Gains from Trade', *Journal of Political Economy*, **89**, pp. 959–73.

Krugman, P. (1985), 'A "Technology Gap" Model of International Trade', in K. Jungenfert and D. Hague (eds), *Structural Adjustment in Developed Open Economies*, New York: St. Martin's Press, pp. 35–49.

Krugman, P. (1987), 'The Narrow Moving Band, the Dutch Disease, and the Competitive Consequences of Mrs. Thatcher', *Journal of Development Economics*, **27**, pp. 41–55.

Krugman, P. (1990), *Rethinking International Trade*, Cambridge, MA: MIT Press.

Kumar, N. and N.S. Siddharthan (1994), 'Technology, Firm Size and Export Behaviour in Developing Countries: The Case of Indian Enterprise', *Journal of Development Studies*, **32** (2), pp. 288–309.

Lancaster, K. (1980), 'Intra-industry trade under Perfect Monopolistic Competition', *Journal of International Economics*, **10**, pp. 151–75.

Landesmann, M. and A. Snell (1989), 'The Consequences of Mrs Thatcher for UK Manufacturing Exports', *Economic Journal*, **99**, pp. 1–27.

Leamer, E. (1974), 'The Commodity Composition of International Trade in Manufactures: An Empirical Analysis', *Oxford Economic Papers*, **26**, pp. 350–74.

Leamer, E. (1980), 'The Leontief Paradox Reconsidered', *Journal of Political Economy*, **88**, pp. 495–503.

Leontief, W. (1953), 'Domestic Production and Foreign Trade: The American Capital Position Re-examined', *Proceedings of the American Philosophical Society*, September, pp. 332–49.

Lin, T. and P. Schmidt (1984), 'A Test of the Tobit Specification Against an Alternative Suggested by Cragg', *Review of Economics and Statistics*, **66**, pp. 174–7.

Linder, S. (1961), *An Essay in Trade and Transformation*, New York: Wiley.

Lundberg, L. (1988), 'Technology, Factor Proportions and Competitiveness', *Scandinavian Journal of Economics*, **90** (2), pp. 173–88.

Lundvall, B.A. (ed.) (1992), *National Systems of Innovation: Towards a Theory of Innovation and Interactive learning*, London: Pinter.

Lyons, B. (1989), 'An Empirical Investigation of UK Manufacturing's Trade with the World and the E.E.C.: 1968 and 1980', in D. Audretsch, L. Sleuwaegen and H. Yamawaki (eds), *The Convergence of International and Domestic Markets*, Amsterdam: North-Holland, pp. 155–87.

Maddison, A. (1991), *Dynamic Forces in Capitalist Development. A Long-Run Comparative View*, Oxford: Oxford University Press.

Magnier, A. and J. Toujas-Bernate (1994), 'Technology and Trade: Empirical Evidences from the Major Five Industrialized Countries', *Weltwirtschaftliches Archiv*, **130** (3), pp. 494–520.

Mansfield, E. (1981), 'Composition of R&D Expenditures: Relationship to Size of Firm, Concentration and Innovative Output', *Review of Economics and Statistics*, **63**, pp. 610–15.

Maskus, K., C. Sveikauskus, and A. Webster (1994), 'The Composition of the Human Capital Stock and its Relation to International Trade: Evidence from the US and Britain', *Weltwirtshaftiches Archiv*, **130** (1), pp. 50–76.

Momigliano, F. and D. Siniscalco (1984), 'Specializazione Internazionale, Technologia e Caratteristiche dell'Offerta' [International Specialisation, Technology and the Characteristics of Supply], *Moneta e Credito*, **XXXVII**, pp. 121–66.

Mowery, D.C. (1992), 'The Challenges of International Trade to U.S. Technology Policy', in M.C. Harris and G.E. Moore (eds), *Linking Trade and Technology Policies: An International Comparison of the Policies of Industrialised Nations*, Washington D.C: National Academy Press, pp. 103–15.

Narula, R. (1995), *Multinational Investment and Economic Structure*, London: Routledge.

Nelson, R.R. (1992), 'What is "Commercial" and What is "Public" about Technology, and What Should Be?', in N. Rosenberg, R. Landau and D. Mowery (eds), *Technology and the Wealth of Nations*, Stanford: Stanford University Press, pp. 57–72.

Nelson, R.R. (ed.) (1993), *National Innovation Systems: A Comparative Analysis*, Oxford: Oxford University Press.

Nelson, R.R. and S. Winter (1974), 'Neoclassical Versus Evolutionary Theories of Economic Growth: Critique and Prospectus', *Economic Journal*, **84**, pp. 886–905.

Nelson, R.R. and S. Winter (1982), *An Evolutionary Theory of Economic Change*, Cambridge, MA: Harvard University Press.

OECD (1986), *Science and Technology Indicators: No. 2 R&D, Invention and Competitiveness*, Paris: OECD.

Oulton, N. (1996), 'Workforce Skills and Export Performance: An Anglo-German Comparison', in Alison L. Booth and Dennis J. Snower (eds), *Acquiring Skills: Market Failures, their Symptoms and Policy Responses*, Cambridge: Cambridge University Press, pp. 199–230.

Owen, N. (1983*), Economies of Scale, Competitiveness and Trade Patterns in the EC*, London: Pinter.

Patel, P. and K. Pavitt (1987), 'Is Western Europe Losing the Technological Race?', *Research Policy*, **16**, pp. 59–85.

Patel, P. and K. Pavitt (1991), 'Large Firms in the Production of the World's Technology: An Important Case of Non-globalisation', *Journal of International Business Studies*, **22** (1), pp. 1–21.

Pavitt, K. (1982), 'R&D, Patenting and Innovative Activities: A Statistical Exploration', *Research Policy*, **11**, pp. 33–51.

Pavitt, K (1984), 'Sectoral Patterns of Technical Change: Towards a Taxonomy and a Theory', *Research Policy*, **13** (6), pp. 343–73.

Pavitt, K. (1985), 'Patent Statistics as Indicators of Innovative Activities: Possibilities and Problems', *Scientometrics*, **7**, pp. 77–99.

Pavitt, K., M. Robson and J. Townsend (1987), 'The Size Distribution of Innovating Firms in the UK: 1945–1983', *Journal of Industrial Economics*, **XXXV**, pp. 297–316.

Pavitt, K. and L. Soete (1980), 'Innovative Activities and Export Shares: Some Comparisons between Industries and Countries', in K. Pavitt (ed.), *Technical Innovation and British Economic Performance*, London: Macmillan, pp. 38-66.

Penrose, E. (1958), *The Theory of the Growth of the Firm*, Oxford: Basil Blackwell.

Peretto, P. (1990), 'Technology, Learning Opportunity and International Competitiveness: Some Empirical Evidence with Panel Data', *Giornale degli Economisti e Annali di Economia*, **49**, pp. 219–44.

Posner, M. (1961), 'International Trade and Technical Change', *Oxford Economic Papers*, **XIII**, pp. 323–41.

Robson, M., J. Townsend and K. Pavitt (1988), 'Sectoral Patterns of Production and Use of Innovations in the UK: 1945–1983', *Research Policy*, **17**, pp. 1–14.

Romer, P. (1990), 'Endogenous Technological Change', *Journal of Political Economy*', **98**, pp. s71–s102.

Rosenberg, N. (1976), *Perspectives on Technology*, Cambridge: Cambridge University Press.

Rosenberg, N. (1982), *Inside the Black Box*, Cambridge: Cambridge University Press.

Scherer, F.M. (1965), 'Firm Size, Market Structure, Opportunity, and the Output of Patented Inventions', *American Economic Review*, **55**, pp. 1097–125.

Scherer, F.M. (1982), 'Demand Pull and Technological Invention: Schmookler Revisited', *The Journal of Industrial Economics*, **XXX** (3), pp. 225–37.

Scherer, F.M. (1983), 'The Propensity to Patent', *International Journal of Industrial Organisation*, **1**, pp. 107–28.

Scherer, F.M. (1984), 'Using Linked Patent and R&D Data to Measure Inter-industry Technology Flows', in Z. Griliches (ed.), *R&D, Patents and Productivity*, Chicago: Chicago University Press, pp. 417–61.

Schumpeter, J. (1934), *The Theory of Economic Development*, Cambridge, MA: Harvard University Press.

Schumpeter, J. (1939), *Business Cycles*, Cambridge, MA: Harvard University Press.

Schumpeter, J. (1943), *Capitalism, Socialism and Democracy*, New York: Harper & Brothers,.

Silverberg, G., G. Dosi, and L. Orsenigo (1988), 'Innovation, Diversity and Diffusion: A Self Organisation Model', *Economic Journal*, **98**, pp. 1032–54.

Simon, H. (1986), 'On the Behavioural and Rational Foundations of Economics Dynamics', in R. Day and G. Eliasson (eds), *The Dynamics of Market Economies*, Amsterdam: North-Holland, pp. 21–44.

Simonetti, R. (1994), 'Technological Change and Firm Growth: "Creative Destruction" in the Fortune List', Paper presented at the Schumpeter Society Conference, Munster, August.

Soete, L. (1981), 'A General Test of Technological Gap Trade Theory', *Weltwirtschaftliches Archiv*, **117**, pp. 638–59.

Soete, L. (1987), 'The Impact of Technological Innovation on International Trade Patterns: The Evidence Reconsidered', *Research Policy*, **16**, pp. 101–30.

Soete, L. (1990), 'Technical Change Theory and International Trade Competition', in J. de la Mothe and L. Ducharme (eds), *Science, Technology and Free Trade*, London: Pinter, pp. 9–18.

Soete, L. and B. Verspagen (1992), 'Technology and Growth: The Complex Dynamics of Catching Up, Falling Behind and Taking Over', in A. Szirmai, B. van Ark, and D. Pilat (eds), *Explaining Economic Growth*, Amsterdam: North-Holland, pp. 101–27.

Soete, L. and B. Verspagen (1994), 'Competing for Growth: The Dynamics of Technology Gaps', in L.L. Pasinetti and R.M. Solow (eds), *Economic Growth and the Structure of Long Term Development*, London: St. Martin's Press, pp. 272–99.

Soete, L. and S. Wyatt (1983), 'The Use of Foreign Patenting as an Internationally Comparable Science and Technology Output Indicator', *Scientometrics*, **5**, pp. 31–45.

Stern, R. and K. Maskus (1981), 'Determinants of the Structure of US Foreign Trade 1958–76', *Journal of International Economics*, **11**, pp. 207–24.

Sveikaukus, L. (1983), 'Science and Technology in US Foreign Trade', *The Economic Journal*, **93**, pp. 542–54.

Teece, D. (1986), 'Profiting from Technological Innovation', *Research Policy*, **15** (6), pp. 285–305.

Temple, P. (1994), 'The Evolution of UK Trading Performance' in T. Buxton, P. Chapman and P. Temple (eds), *Britain's Economic Performance*, London: Routledge, pp. 76–97.

Thirlwall, A. (1986), *Balance of Payments Theory and the UK Experience*, 3rd edn, London: Macmillan.

Tyson, d'Andrea L. (1992), *Who's Bashing Whom? Trade Conflict in High-Technology Industries*, Washington DC: Institute for International Economics.

University of Sussex, Science Policy Research Unit (1982*), Innovations in the UK since 1945*, Colchester: ESRC Data Archive.

van Hulst, N., R. Mulder and L. Soete (1991), 'Exports and Technology in Manufacturing Industry', *Weltwirtschaftliches Archiv*, **127** (2), pp. 246–64.

Vernon, V. (1966), 'International Investment and International Trade in the Product Cycle', *Quarterly Journal of Economics*, **LXXX**, pp. 190–207.

Verspagen, B. (1993), *Uneven Growth between Interdependent Economies*, Aldershot: Avebury.

Verspagen, B. and K. Wakelin (1997a), 'International Competitiveness and its Determinants', *International Journal of Applied Economics*, **11** (2), pp. 177–90.

Verspagen, B. and K. Wakelin (1997b), 'Technology, Employment and Trade: Perspectives on European Convergence', in J. Fagerberg, A. Melchoir, L. Lundberg and P. Hansson (eds), *Technology and International Trade*, Cheltenham, UK: Edward Elgar, pp. 56–74.

Vestal, J.E. (1989), 'Evidence on the Determinants and Factor Content Characteristics of Japanese Technology Trade, 1977–1982', *Review of Economics and Statistics*, **71**, pp. 565–71.

Walker, W. (1979), *Industrial Innovation and International Trading Performance*, Greenwich, CT: JAI Press.

Walker, W. (1993), 'National Systems of Innovation: Britain', in R.R. Nelson (ed.), *National Innovation Systems: A Comparative Analysis*, Oxford: Oxford University Press, pp. 158–91.

Wells, L. (ed.) (1972), *Product Life Cycle and International Trade*, Cambridge, MA: Harvard University Press.

Willmore, Larry (1992), 'Transnationals and Foreign Trade: Evidence from Brazil', *The Journal of Development Studies*, **28** (2), pp. 314–35.

Wood, A. (1994), 'Give Heckscher and Ohlin a Chance!', *Weltwirtschaftliches Archiv*, **130** (1), pp. 20–49.

Yoffie, D.B. (1992), 'Technology Challenges to Trade Policy', in M.C. Harris and G.E. Moore (eds), *Linking Trade and Technology Policies: An International Comparison of the Policies of Industrialised Nations*, Washington DC: National Academy Press, pp. 116–31.

Index